About this Skills Book

This book is designed to help you develop your skills in reading, writing, spelling, punctuation and grammar. These skills are very important in everyday life, and having a greater understanding of them should increase your confidence, help you to fulfil your potential, and give you more control over what you choose to do with your life. Achieving a Level 1 qualification in Adult Literacy will prove that you have developed your knowledge and skills to this standard.

This Skills Book will help you to pass the Level 1 Adult Literacy test by helping you develop exactly those skills that you need for the test. This means that you'll take the test feeling more comfortable and more confident that you can succeed. Here's how:

■ **Section A: Ways of reading**
Develop different reading skills by **scanning** for key words, **skimming** to work out what a text is about, and **reading in detail**.

■ **Section B: Understanding how texts are organised**
Learn to recognise **different types of text**, from letters to reports and tables. Understand and use **different features of texts**.

■ **Section C: Understanding what writers want their readers to do**
Find out about how texts give **instructions**, **describe** something, **explain** something or **persuade** the reader.

■ **Section D: Spelling words correctly**
Get lots of tips for **improving your spelling** plus plenty of practice in spotting and correcting spelling mistakes.

■ **Section E: Using punctuation correctly**
Find out how to make your meaning clear by **using punctuation correctly**, including capital letters, full stops, exclamation marks, question marks and commas.

■ **Section F: Using good grammar**
Learn to **use correct grammar**, e.g. getting verb tenses right and making sure the subject and verb of a sentence agree.

■ **Section G: Preparing for the test**
Finally pull all your skills together and make sure you are **ready for the test**, with practice in reading and answering the different types of question.

How to use this book

Each section starts with a short explanation, followed by a wide range of activities to help you understand the skill. Each section ends with a short test, and you can record your scores in the chart at the back of this book to see your own progress.

Most people find some of the skills easier to master than others, and the Teacher's Handbook has practice sheets to go with each skill so you get plenty of support with anything you find difficult. This symbol 24 at the end of each section tells you which pages of the Teacher's Handbook to refer to. There is also a Hot Topics CD-ROM with games to help you enjoy practising your skills, and your teacher will have a Practice Tests CD-ROM to help you revise for the test.

It's as simple as that. Get ready to feel your confidence improve. Good luck and enjoy developing new skills.

A Ways of reading

By the end of this section you should be able to read in different ways to obtain information from texts. You will know how to:

▷▷ scan for key words

▷▷ skim for a general idea of what a text is about

▷▷ read in detail for greater understanding.

You will then test out your mastery of these skills at the end of the section.

1 Scanning for key words

▌▌ *First read this ...*

You scan when you search for something you need to find out.

■ Search for key words by moving your eyes quickly over the page.

■ You don't need to read every word.

▶▶ *Now try it!*

1 *Before* you scan a text, decide which important words you need to search for (the key words). The table below lists three tasks. For each task, list three key words or phrases that you would search for. The first one has been done for you.

A Search a DVD cover to check if it is a funny film.	*crying with laughter funny hilarious*
B Search a CD cover to make sure it is your favourite music.	
C Search a pizza menu for your favourite pizza.	

2 (Circle) words in the box below that would help you to find
   a vegetarian pizza.

   | chicken   vegetarian   onion   pepper   tuna |
   | beef   mushroom   sweetcorn   pepperoni |
   | pineapple   chilli   tomato   ham   olive |

3 Underline words in the box above that would tell you
   that a pizza is not vegetarian.

4 Scan the menu below and find four vegetarian pizzas.
   Underline their names.

		MED	LARGE	MEGA
1	**CHEESE AND TOMATO**	£6.75	£8.95	£11.50
2	**SICILIAN** *Ham, anchovies, artichokes, garlic*	£6.75	£8.95	£11.50
3	**NAPOLITANA** *Pepperoni*	£6.75	£8.95	£11.50
4	**HAWAIIAN** *Ham and pineapple* NEW!	£6.75	£8.95	£11.50
5	**PERFECT PEPPERONI** *Pepperoni and mozzarella*	£6.75	£8.95	£11.50
6	**PEPPERONI FEAST** *Double pepperoni, red onion*	£6.75	£8.95	£11.50
7	**TASTY CHICKEN** *Mexican chicken, mushroom, sweetcorn*	£6.75	£8.95	£11.50
8	**BBQ CHICKEN** *Chicken, BBQ sauce, red onion, red peppers*	£6.75	£8.95	£11.50
9	**FRUITS OF THE SEA** *Tuna, anchovies, mussels, prawns*	£6.75	£8.95	£11.50
10	**MEAT MOUNTAIN** *Chilli beef, salami, meatballs, spicy pork*	£6.75	£8.95	£11.50
11	**ITALIAN BURNOUT** *Beef, red onion, chillies*	£6.75	£8.95	£11.50
12	**FEEL THE HEAT** *Tandoori chicken, green chillies, red onion* NEW! ...	£6.75	£8.95	£11.50
13	**BANANA CHICKEN** *Chicken, banana, mushroom*	£6.75	£8.95	£11.50
14	**VEGETARIAN** *Fresh tomatoes, green peppers, courgettes, red onion*	£6.75	£8.95	£11.50
15	**VEGGIE DELUXE** *Red onion, mushroom, sweetcorn, fresh tomatoes*	£6.75	£8.95	£11.50
16	**FOUR CHEESES** *Gorgonzola, parmesan, mozzarella, gruyere cheeses*	£6.75	£8.95	£11.50

5 You need to find three pizzas that taste hot and spicy. First
   note the key words that will help your search. Then scan
   the pizza menu for them and (circle) the pizzas' names.

Write your key words here:

chilli
spicy

6 How many pizzas have the topping ingredients that are
   listed below? Count as you scan the menu.
   Record your answers in this chart.

Topping	In how many pizzas?
Chicken	
Mushroom	
Red onion	
Sweetcorn	
Pineapple	

Test tip

Scan a text when a question
asks you to look for particular
information, such as a name,
number or place.

2 Skimming to find out what a text is about

First read this ...

You skim a text when you need an overview of what it is about and what the writer is trying to do (e.g. persuade, explain or describe).

■ Read the text quickly. You don't need to read every word.

■ Keep pausing to ask yourself: *'What is this about?'*
'Why has it been written?'

Now try it!

1   Skim voucher A below. Then tick the statement that best sums up what the text is about.

A   Someone giving you money to buy a DVD. ☐

B   Someone inviting you to watch a DVD with them. ☐

C   Being able to rent as many DVDs as you like for a month. ☐

A

£10   **SCREEN★SELECT**
the new way to rent DVDs   £10

Gift Voucher

To: Isobel

0 24750 000 586610

Try out this great DVD rental service. This voucher gives you 1 month's unlimited DVD rental, delivered to your door. I use them and really recommend it. Enjoy!
(See over for how to redeem)

From: Jack

1 month unlimited DVD rental

the new way to rent DVDs

B

This voucher entitles you to 1 month of unlimited DVD rental delivered to your door from ScreenSelect.co.uk.

How it works

1. Select	2. Receive	3. Watch	4. Swap
Choose online from the UK's largest selection	**Get** your DVDs by 1st class post	**Keep** as long as you like – no late fees	**Post** back FREE & we'll send you more

How to claim

Visit www.screenselect.co.uk
and enter gift code: **MG30**

2   Skim voucher B. Then tick the statement that tells you what the writer wants you to do.

A   Visit a new DVD shop. ☐

B   Buy DVDs online. ☐

C   Visit the Screen Select website to get your free DVD rental. ☐

D   Visit the Screen Select website to see if there are any DVDs you like. ☐

3 Skim the texts below. Then read statements A to F. Draw a line to join up each text with the statement that best sums up what it is about.

Daisy is Missing.
My black and white kitten has a green collar. She was last seen on Wed 3rd January in Waterman Street. Please call Mike on 07833 53432 if you find her.

A How to enter a competition to answer questions about football.

B How to make sweetcorn soup.

C Mike wants to know if you have found his missing cat.

D How to cook cobs of corn.

E If you find the missing cat you will get a reward.

F How to enter a competition to win the chance to watch the FA Cup Final.

Corn on the cob

Place cobs in a saucepan of boiling water. Do <u>not</u> add any salt because this makes the corn tough. Add a pinch of sugar and boil for 8 minutes or until tender. Serve immediately with butter and salt and pepper.

Be there!

You could win tickets to watch the *FA Cup Final!* Simply text us or call with the answer to the following question:

Who scored the winning goal in the 2006 World Cup?

Text or phone your answer to *07098 456324.*
(All calls cost £1)

Test tip

Be careful if you are answering a multiple-choice question using skimming. One answer will be right but the others might be *nearly* right. Carefully read and test out each possible answer before you make your choice.

3 Reading carefully for detailed understanding

▮▮ **First read this ...**

Reading carefully gives you a detailed understanding of what a writer is saying in a text, or what several details in a text add up to.

- ■ Decide what you need to find out. Next skim the whole text, including headings, to gain an overview. Then scan to find the parts of the text you need to read carefully.

- ■ Read every word in those sentences carefully. Stop at the end of each sentence and ask yourself: *'What did it tell me?'*

- ■ If you don't understand what a word or detail means, reread the whole sentence again and try to work it out.

▶▶ Now try it!

1 Carefully read this website page. What kind of guests are the makers of the show looking for? Draw a line from each true statement below to the text in the website that tells you this.

- A Confident people who like acting.

- B People who enjoy discussing things calmly.

- C People with strong views and who speak their mind.

- D People who will get angry about things but don't mind being famous.

News

Big Brother: Big Brother's Big Mouth is Back

Thursday 18 May
Day 1, 22:00

Fronted by Russell Brand, it's bigger, it's better and you can catch it on <u>E4</u> four nights a week.

Do <u>you love</u> nothing better than <u>a good argument</u>? Do you want the opportunity to <u>enforce your opinions</u> on the rest of the nation? <u>Do you say what you like, and like what you say</u>? Do you want to be part of the <u>most talked about TV show of 2006</u>? If your answer is Yes, apply to be on the show today!

➡ news home

2 Read the text below. Answer the question: 'What is Big Brother doing to support charities in 2006 and who are they helping?' Put a tick in the box against the correct answer.

A Big Brother is giving 10p of every vote cast to two charities, Shelter and Teenage Cancer Trust. ☐

B Big Brother is making a donation to charity which will be divided between Shelter (which helps people find and keep a home and campaigns for decent housing for all), Teenage Cancer Trust (which provides specialist units for teenagers) and a third charity to be chosen by the winner. ☐

C Big Brother is giving 10p of every vote cast that will be divided between Shelter (which helps people find and keep a home and campaigns for decent housing for all), Teenage Cancer Trust (which provides specialist units for teenagers), and a third charity chosen by Channel 4. ☐

D Big Brother is giving 10p of every vote cast that will be divided between Shelter (which helps people find and keep a home and campaigns for decent housing for all), Teenage Cancer Trust (which provides specialist units for teenagers), and a third charity chosen by voters. ☐

Test tip

Close reading is very important in the test. Using it will help you to understand properly what the question is asking. It will also help you to understand fully what you need to in the text, and be really sure that the answer you tick is right.

Charities

Raise Money for Charity During Big Brother 2006

This year, 10p of every vote cast during Big Brother will be divided between three charities: Shelter, Teenage Cancer Trust and a third to be chosen by the series winner.

Shelter

Shelter
Shelter believes everyone should have a home. We help more than 170,000 people a year fight for their rights, get back on their feet, and find and keep a home. We also tackle the root causes of bad housing by campaigning for new laws, policies, and solutions...
>more

Teenage Cancer Trust
Each day in the UK, six teenagers will find out they have cancer. Teenage Cancer Trust focuses on the needs of teenagers and young adults with cancer by providing specialist teenage units in NHS hospitals, as well as UK-wide education and awareness to educate teenagers about the disease...
>more

4 Working out what a word means

What do you do when you need to work out what a word means?

■ **Stop** when you read the word that you need to understand.

■ **Ask yourself** these three questions:
  1 What is the rest of the **paragraph** about?
  2 What is the **sentence** that this word is in about?
  3 What **other words would make sense** instead of this word?

▶▶ Now try it!

1 Which of the answers below means the same as the word in bold in the paragraph?

A change ☐   B bill ☐   C money back ☐

> If a customer wants their money back, try the camera yourself to see if it works. Check carefully to see if there are any marks or signs of damage. <u>We do not give any **refunds** if the camera has not been treated properly, e.g. if it looks as if it has become wet or been dropped.</u>

This **paragraph** is about *when a customer can be given their money back*.

The **sentence** is about *not doing something if the camera has been badly treated*.

2 You are going to work out what the word in bold in the paragraph below means.

So the **word** is about *getting your money back*.

> Before you start to make popcorn, get everything ready. <u>Make sure that you have all the cooking **utensils** you need, including a spoon, a saucepan with a lid and a bowl.</u> Make sure that the lid of your saucepan fits tightly, or your popcorn may escape while you are cooking!

a) First read the paragraph above, then tick the right statements below and on page 11.

The paragraph is about:

A eating popcorn ☐

B tidying the kitchen ☐

C making popcorn. ☐

The sentence is about:

A choosing a saucepan ☐

B collecting all the tools you need ☐

C finding the ingredients. ☐

b) The answer below that means the same as 'utensils' is:

A kitchen equipment ☐

B knife and fork ☐

C food. ☐

3 Read the paragraphs below. What do the words in bold mean? <u>Underline</u> the words in the boxes that mean the same as the words in bold.

a)

> This is only a **draft version** of my letter of application. Would you mind checking it for me? Then I can correct any mistakes and print out a final version to send off tomorrow.

| light wind | finished copy | first plan | best effort |

b)

> The experiment did not work because the chemical was **contaminated**. Before we started the experiment, we washed the test tube with soapy water. Unfortunately a small amount of soapy water must have still been in the test tube when we added the chemical. The chemical did not behave as we expected. It could have been the soap or the water that caused this.

| poisonous | wet | not pure | clean |

c)

> I've never really wanted to do any other job. I've always felt I had a **calling** to be a nurse. Some people feel that way about becoming a teacher or a police officer. I think I have wanted to be a nurse ever since I was very small. My mum says I was always bandaging up my teddy bear and giving it medicine.

| happy feeling | strong wish | chance | reason |

5 Identifying the main point

First read this ...

When you need to know the main point of a paragraph, you work it out by skimming and close reading. This helps you to spot the big idea in the paragraph.

■ Skim the whole text, including any headings, to work out what it is about.

■ Read the paragraph in detail and ask yourself: 'What big idea is this text about?'

■ Sum up in a few words what the paragraph is about.

Now try it!

1   Skim the e-mails below. Choose the statement that best sums up what they are about.

A   AJ and Gav are discussing different ways to use hairspray.

B   Gav wants to remove some graffiti and AJ tells him how.

C   Two friends are in touch about the trouble Jed has caused.

Mail Message

Send   Save   Attach file

Help, AJ!
Jed's scribbled graffiti in red marker pen all over the back fence and now Mum says I can't go to the party tonight. How can I get the red off?
Gav

Mail Message

Send   Save   Attach file

Hi Gav
I checked on the internet and a website says spray the fence with loads of hairspray, leave it and then wipe it off. The site says hairspray can remove marker pen stains from fabric, or wooden or painted surfaces. Good luck – if your mum calms down, see you tonight.
AJ

---

2   Read the second e-mail on page 12 in detail. Then tick the statement below which best sums up its main point.

A   Hairspray can be used for other things apart from doing your hair. ☐

B   The internet says use a lot of hairspray so Gav can go to the party. ☐

C   A website says hairspray can be used to remove marker pen stains. ☐

Test tip

Work out the main point when a question asks you to choose a statement that best sums up what a paragraph or text is about. Remember that in a multiple-choice question all the answers *seem* possible but **only one is right.** Make sure you have thought carefully about whether each one is right before making your final choice.

3   Read the text below. Work out the main point of each paragraph in turn. Then write the number of the paragraph next to the statement below that best sums it up.

A   Graffiti can make small businesses leave an area. _____

B   Graffiti can make an area feel depressing. _____

C   Graffiti is expensive because it costs so much to remove it. _____

D   Areas covered with graffiti are likely to become crime hot spots. _____

GRAFFITI

1   Graffiti can spoil people's enjoyment of their local area. Many people find looking at walls that have graffiti and rude messages on them depressing. It is easy to feel that no one cares about the area or that it is 'a bit of a dump' because it looks so bad.

2   Seeing graffiti can also make people feel worried that an area is unsafe. If many people choose not to use areas that have a lot of graffiti then these places end up being empty for much of the time. When someone does walk through them they will feel much more vulnerable, and in fact it is easy for such areas to become hot spots for muggings, vandalism and other anti-social behaviours.

3   Local businesses and local authorities have to clean up graffiti. The problem is so great in some areas that local councils have to employ several people to remove it. Their wages and the materials used have to be paid for out of the Council Tax we all pay. This means that the money cannot be used on other things.

4   Some businesses may choose to move out of an area if it gets a lot of graffiti. This is because firstly, it costs a lot to keep cleaning it up; secondly, customers and staff may feel unsafe in the area and thirdly, the local crime rate may go up. This means that there are fewer jobs for local people and fewer customers for local shops. Very quickly an area can go downhill, and all because of graffiti.

4   Tick the statement below that best sums up the main point of the text above.

A   Graffiti is the result of living in a poor and troubled area. ☐

B   Graffiti can make an area become poorer and more troubled. ☐

6 Identifying a specific detail

First read this ...

When you need to find a specific detail in a text, follow these three steps:

■ **Decide** what you need to find out and **skim** the text to find the place where that information is likely to be.

■ **Scan** the right part of the text for key words to find the sentence you need.

■ **Search** each chunk of the sentence carefully for the detail you want.

Now try it!

1 Skim the advertisement opposite. You need to find out when the course is running in Manchester. Put a cross against the part that tells you when courses run.

2 Now scan that chunk of the advertisement and <u>underline</u> the word 'Manchester'.

3 Read the line that the word 'Manchester' is on and put the date in this sentence:

The course is running in Manchester on _____

_____ .

4 Read paragraphs 1 and 2 of the advertisement and ⊙circle⊙ these details in the text.

   a) How long Simon has worked as a coach for Bobby Robson.

   b) The names of the Republic of Ireland players Simon has worked with.

   c) The name of the company that runs the goalkeeping tour.

   d) The age that people must be to go on the course.

Test tip

In the test, it's a good idea to read the right part of the text several times to check that you have noticed and understood everything that you need to find.

5   Read paragraph 4. Which of these skills will **not** be taught
     on the course?

   A Warm ups and footwork.

   B Tackling and scoring.

   C Crossing and dealing with the back pass.

   D Handling and shot stopping.

Goalkeeping coaching

Simon Smith is one of the country's
leading goalkeeping coaches. Simon
spent six seasons as Sir Bobby Robson's
Goalkeeping Coach at Newcastle United
5   F.C., working with the Republic of Ireland's
Shay Given and Stephen Harper before
moving abroad to work as a consultant
to the Canadian Soccer Association.

This is the sixth year Simon Smith
10 Goalkeeping has run its national
goalkeeping tour giving boys and girls
between the ages of 8–18 the opportunity
to train as the professionals do with coaches dedicated to improving techniques
and skills and ultimately improving match day performance.

15 These courses allow you to learn and fine-tune all the techniques and skills you
require to become a top class goalkeeper – the rest is up to you!

The course will cover the main techniques and skills of goalkeeping: goalkeeping
specific warm ups, handling, footwork, diving, shot stopping, one v one crossing,
dealing with the back pass, distribution; these topics will be covered in realistic
20 match related practices giving you the edge when you return to the team.

Course dates:

27th May (Saturday)   Coventry (Alan Higgs Sports Centre)
28th May (Sunday)   London (Metropolitan Police Club, Chigwell)
29th May (Monday)   Manchester (Egerton Youth Club, Knutsford)
25 30th May (Tuesday)   Newcastle (venue to be confirmed)

To find out more about these and other courses run by Simon Smith Goalkeeping
or to request an application form, call 0191 2526950 or log on to:

www.simonsmithgoalkeeping.com

7 Test your skills

Use the test below to find out how well you have mastered the skills in Section A.

These questions are all about the text opposite.

1   The main point of the text opposite is:

A ☐   to tell you where to buy henna

B ☐   to tell you which countries mehndi comes from

C ☐   to explain about mehndi for people who do not know what it is

D ☐   to encourage you to try mehndi at home.

2   Read the first paragraph. Mehndi is carried out:

A ☐   at funerals and christenings

B ☐   as part of the traditional celebration of birthdays

C ☐   traditionally to celebrate special occasions

D ☐   only by women.

3   Read the second paragraph. Henna comes from:

A ☐   reddish-orange mud

B ☐   the flowers of a plant

C ☐   the young leaves and twigs of a shrub

D ☐   every country across the world.

4   According to the text, which country is henna **not** grown in?

A ☐   India

B ☐   Ireland

C ☐   Pakistan

D ☐   Egypt.

5   Another word with a similar meaning to 'traditional' in line 4 is:

A ☐   artistic

B ☐   long-established

C ☐   fashionable

D ☐   unisex.

Test tip

Always read the questions carefully. Some questions in the test are like Question 4 where you have to tick something that is **not** included in the text. You need to search the text very carefully and find the three aspects that **are** in the text. That way you will know for sure what to tick that is **not** included in the text. For more help with this see Section G, page 84.

Check your answers.
How many did you get right?   /5

WHAT IS MEHNDI?

Mehndi is the art of applying Henna on the body. It is a beautiful form of temporary body decoration. Mehndi is a traditional form of decoration for both men and women in countries such as India, Morocco and Pakistan. It is generally used for special occasions, particularly weddings.

line 1
line 2
line 3
line 4
line 5
line 6
line 7
line 8

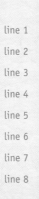

HOW IS HENNA DYE MADE?

Henna is a small shrub called *Lawsonia inermis*, and is found in Iran, India, Pakistan, Egypt and North Africa. The young leaves and twigs are ground into a fine powder, then mixed with water and applied on the hands, feet and hair to give them a reddish-orange colour. The henna mud mixture can be applied in beautiful patterns via a small plastic bag with a small hole pricked into one corner. This bag acts as a mini cake-decorating tube.

line 9
line 10
line 11
line 12
line 13
line 14
line 15
line 16
line 17
line 18

B Understanding how texts are organised

By the end of this section you will understand how writers use different formats and features in different kinds of texts. You will know how to:

▶▶ recognise different formats and their purposes, e.g. letters, e-mails, reports, charts and images

▶▶ understand how features help to organise texts

▶▶ work out what kind of text you are reading and where you will find the information you need.

You will then test these skills at the end of the section.

1 Recognising different features in texts

First read this ...

When you first read a text:

■ remember what different features a text can have

■ skim the text so that you see how it is organised, what the features are and what the different parts are telling you.

This will help you to understand it better.

Test tip

In the test, different kinds of text are often called documents. They include letters, memos and newspaper and magazine articles.

Now try it!

1 Skim texts A to F on page 19. Then write the right letter in the table to show which text is which text type. Next, fill in the table to show which features are in each text. The first column is done for you.

Feature	Tells readers	E-mail B	Letter	Memo	Instruction	Chart	Advert
Main heading	This is the main idea of the whole text.	✓					
Subheading	This is the main point of this part of the text.						
Numbering	You need to understand the points in this order.						
Bullet points	These are different points.						
Paragraphs	The sentences in this part are all about the same idea.	✓					

A

Set of 4 mini disco ducks

Light up your bathtub with these super fun flashing disco ducks.

Turn off your bathroom lights for a groovy light show!

B

Send Save Attach file

From: Toby Fair
To: Rafiq Said
Cc:
Subject: You're quackers

Hi mate,

Thanks for leaving all those disco ducks for me to find in my bath at two o'clock in the morning. I thought I was seeing things. I haven't laughed so much in ages.

It's given me a great idea for the office party. Just you wait!

Cheers,

Toby

C

Date: 24 June 2007

To: Midsummer Party Organiser

From: Toby Fair

Subject: How the Disco Duck Race will work

- Everyone will find a disco duck sitting on their chair at the dinner table.
- Each duck will be labelled with its owner's name.
- Races start at 21.30 on the river bank behind the marquee.
- We have some amazing prizes!

D

How to Hold a Disco Duck Race

1 Place all ducks in the water and hold in place until the starter shouts 'Go!'.

2 Let go of your duck. (No pushing allowed.)

3 The first duck to reach the finishing line is the winner.

E

Rainbow Trout Farm
Bait Lane, Seaford, Sussex SF1 3DR

Acorn Electrics   23 June 2007
Oak Road
Seaford
Sussex
SF1 2DS

Dear Sir or Madam

We have found 169 flashing disco ducks on our fish farms over the last two days. I understand from the ducks' labels that they are the property of your company and so I am returning them to you.

Since the ducks' arrival we have had no problems with herons taking our fish. We are now thinking of buying disco ducks to act as 'trout farm scarecrows'.

Yours faithfully

Ivor Catch

F

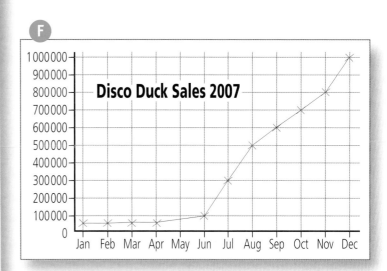

2 Understanding headings, subheadings and points

Writers often use headings, numbered points, bullet points and paragraphs to break up the text. These make it easier for readers to understand the text and find information.
When you read a text:

1 Study the main heading. Ask yourself: *'What big idea is the whole text about?'*

2 Study any subheadings. Ask yourself: *'What is this part of the text going to be about?'*

3 Study the points. Ask yourself: *'How are these organised?'*

▶▶ Now try it!

1 Read the text below. Draw lines to link each of the labels on the right to the relevant part of the text below.

Meeting notes from 3 October 2007

<u>Present:</u> *Jack Boon, Rosh Patel, Taylor Notts, Zara Smith*

1 <u>The office party</u>
  a Date: Friday 20 December or Saturday 21 December.
  b Zara to find suitable venue offering
    • good meal – reasonably priced
    • band or disco
    • somewhere easy to get home from by bus.
  c Taylor to check whether people want to bring partners.

2 <u>Seasonal cards</u>
  a No cards. Jack to make people aware of alternative: putting a message on the board and giving money to charity instead.
  b Organise central message board.
  c Collect donations.

Festive gifts
Rosh to distribute presents on December 21:
Senior Management will get blue and gold packages.
Supervisors will get red and green packages.
All other staff will get yellow and orange packages.

Numbering – points are numbered in the order in which topics were discussed.

Letters are used to show the order in which decisions were made.

Bullet points list what needs to be considered at that stage.

Main heading tells readers that the text is a record of what happened at this meeting.

Subheading tells readers what the subject of the chunk of text that follows is going to be about.

2   Add in the missing numbers, letters, bullets and underlining on the last part of the text on page 20.

3   The text below has been organised in a different way. Look at the list of features below, and draw a line to show where each feature is in the text.

subheading

heading

bullet point

first paragraph

second paragraph

points in time order

points in random order

KARTING MORNING

We hope you are looking forward to our team-building day on Saturday. A map and travel details are attached to this letter.

   Everyone needs to arrive on time so we can get the most out of the morning. There is a café on site so if you can stay on for lunch we could all eat there.

Timetable

9.00 – 9.15 a.m.	Arrive and get dressed in helmets and padding
9.15 – 10.00	What is Kart racing?
10.00 – 10.20	How a Kart works
10.30 – 11.30	Practice runs
11.30 – 12.30	Races

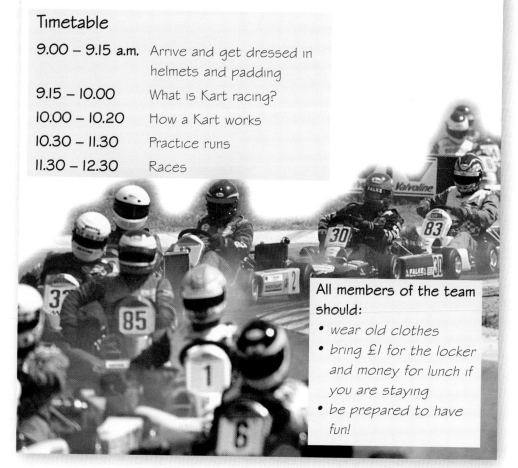

All members of the team should:
- wear old clothes
- bring £1 for the locker and money for lunch if you are staying
- be prepared to have fun!

When you need to search through a list to find information:

- decide whether the headings are in a particular order
  (e.g. order of time, order of importance, alphabetical order)

- check whether the points are in a particular order

- use the order to help you find the information you are looking for.

Now try it!

1 Read the listing opposite. Ring the correct words in the statements below.

A The blue headings are all place names.

They are in random/ alphabetical/ numerical order.

B First the list has in bold print the band's name/ place where the band is playing/ telephone number.

Then the list has the band's name/ place where the band is playing/telephone number.

Last you are told the band's name/ place where the band is playing/ telephone number.

2 When you have found out how a list is organised, you can find information in it more quickly. Use what you know about this list to find the information below.

a) Circle the two bands you can see in Brighton. (One is already done for you.)

b) Underline the three bands you could go and see in Belfast.

c) Underline the telephone number of Café Drummond in Aberdeen.

d) Underline the venue in Cambridge where Mogwai is playing.

TUESDAY April 4

ABERDEEN

Mistakes In Animation / Amber / Steven Milne / Rory McIntyre/ Lindsay Allison *Café Drummond 01224 624642*

Robert Love / Sandy Dillon & Jeff Klein *Moshulu 01224 642662*

Thee More Shallows / Ral Partha / Vogelbacher / The Boy Lacks Patience *The Tunnels 01224 211121*

BELFAST

Rescue The Astronauts / The Winding Stair / Amoruza *Auntie Annies 028 9050 1660*

BIRMINGHAM

Ben Calvert / The Jack Stafford Foundation / Meredust / James Summerfield *Barfly 0870 907 0999*

Hundred Reasons / 65 Days of Static *Carling Academy 2 0121 262 3000*

Pure Reason Revolution *Carling Bar Academy 0121 262 3000*

BRIGHTON

Graham Coxon *Concorde 2 01273 624343*

Hope Of The States *Audio 01273 624343*

BRISTOL

The Concretes *Carling Academy 0870 771 2000*

Flylow / Cobra Kai *Fleece 0117 945 0996*

The Maccabees *Louisiana 0117 926 5978*

CAMBRIDGE

Mogwai *Junction 01223 511511*

CARDIFF

Vito / The Voices *Clwb Ifor Bach 029 2023 2199*

3 The dictionary page below is another kind of list. Explore how it has been organised. Use what you find out to answer the activities below.

a) Circle the first meaning of 'backing'.

b) Circle the word that means 'a bag that you carry on your back while walking'.

c) Underline the musical meaning that backing can have.

d) Circle the word that means: 'a person's family and education'.

back *adverb* to where someone or something has come from, e.g. *We all went back into the living room.*

back *verb* (**backs**, **backing**, **backed**) **1** to move backwards **2** to support someone or give them help.

backbone *noun* (plural **backbones**) the bones down your back, the spine.

background *noun* (plural **backgrounds**) **1** the part of a scene or picture that looks furthest away **2** the things that happened before an event and help to explain it **3** a person's family and education.

backing *noun* **1** support or help **2** a musical accompaniment, especially for a singer.

backpack *noun* (plural **backpacks**) a bag that you carry on your back while walking or travelling.

4 Read the TV listings below. Decide how the information is organised. Use what you find out to help with the activities below.

a) How many animal racing programmes can you watch? _____

b) Circle the three different times that you can watch wrestling.

6.00 a.m.	Race World – horse racing from USA
7.00	Yachting
7.30	Football League
9.00	Racing News – highlights of yesterday's horse racing from Aintree
10.00	Wrestling
1.00 p.m.	Boxing
3.00	Australian Rugby League
5.00	Wrestling
8.00	Greyhounds – racing from White City
10.00	Wrestling

c) At what time can greyhound racing be watched? _____

d) Underline two sports that are broadcast from countries other than Britain.

First read this ...

Information is sometimes presented in charts or tables. Some tables are text based and others contain numbers. When a table organises information into columns and rows:

- read the headings to find out how information is organised, e.g. the heading of each row and column in a table

- decide what you need to find out and where it will be, e.g. the right row or column to search along

- move your finger along or across the table and keep scanning until you find the right information.

Now try it!

1 Tables can help organise information so that it is easier to find. Search the table below to find information on charity singles. The first question has been answered for you.

a) Circle the artists who released the single called 'A Night to Remember'.

b) Circle the charity that benefited from McFly's record.

c) Circle the month when the One World Project released their single.

d) Circle the song that benefited the most charities.

e) Circle the two artists whose songs reached number 1 in the UK charts.

columns

Notable charity singles

rows

Release date	Title	Artists	Charity/Cause	Highest chart position
February 2005	Grief Never Grows Old	One World Project	2004 Asian Tsunami relief	4 (UK)
February 2005	Evie Parts 1, 2 and 3	The Wrights	Stevie Wright, The Salvation Army and 2004 Asian Tsunami relief	2 (Australia)
March 2005	All About You/You've Got A Friend	McFly	Comic Relief	1 (UK)
March 2005	Is This the Way to Amarillo?	Tony Christie featuring Peter Kay	Comic Relief	1 (UK)
November 2005	A Night To Remember	Liberty X	Children in Need	6 (UK)

(source: Wikipedia)

2   By making information more visual, pie charts can make it easier to understand and find the information you need. Using the pie chart, tick the statements below that are true.

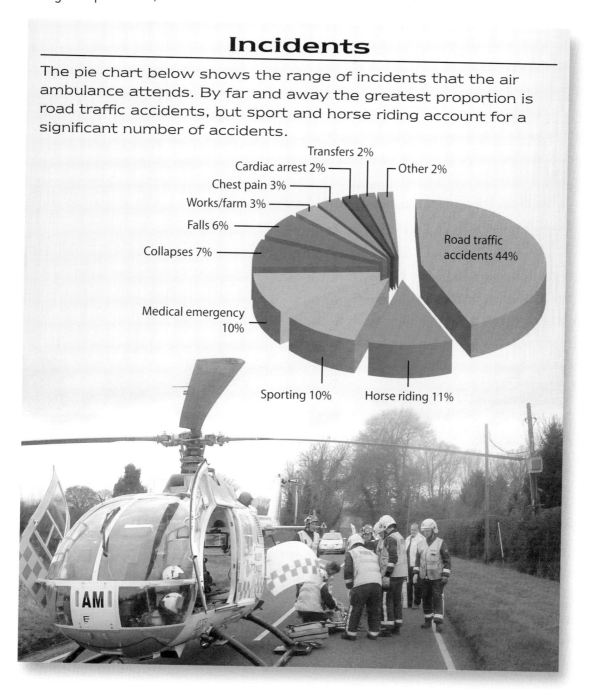

Incidents

The pie chart below shows the range of incidents that the air ambulance attends. By far and away the greatest proportion is road traffic accidents, but sport and horse riding account for a significant number of accidents.

Transfers 2%
Cardiac arrest 2%
Chest pain 3%
Works/farm 3%
Falls 6%
Collapses 7%
Other 2%
Road traffic accidents 44%
Medical emergency 10%
Sporting 10%   Horse riding 11%

A   The air ambulance attends an equal number of collapses and falls.

B   The air ambulance attends more medical emergencies than cardiac arrests.

C   The air ambulance attends fewer falls than transfers.

D   The air ambulance helps more people injured while horse riding than people injured at work or on a farm.

E   The air ambulance is called out to road traffic accidents more than any other incident.

Test tip

- Remember, in a pie chart, the larger the 'slice', the bigger the number.

- Always look carefully when the 'slices' are of a similar size, and make sure you know what each 'slice' represents.

3 The timetable below shows that the 12.00 train from Eastgate arrives in Goban at 12.20. Use the timetable to find the information needed below. The first question has been answered for you.

Stations	Train times			
Eastgate	12.00	12.30	13.00	13.30
Transfold	12.05	12.35	13.05	13.35
Dirsley	12.13	12.43	13.13	13.43
Goban	12.20	12.50	13.20	13.50

Test tip

It often helps to move your finger along the rows and down the columns of a timetable to find the information you need. Read the question very carefully and move your finger from the station or train time where you start to the station or time where you want to end up.

a) Circle the time that a train leaves Transfold after 13.00.

b) Circle the time that the train leaving Transfold at 13.05 arrives in Goban.

c) Put a cross by the time that the train leaving Eastgate at 13.30 arrives in Dirsley.

d) Tick the time of the train from Dirsley that reaches Goban at 12.50.

e) Put a star by the time that the 12.00 train from Eastgate reaches Dirsley.

4 Charts and tables can also help you to compare information. Search the table below to compare the costs of different mobile phones and answer the questions below.

a) How much does one text cost with **Enjoy!** Super tariff? _____

b) How much does a minute's call cost with Extra tariff? _____

c) How much does one text cost with Standard tariff? _____

d) How much does calling your favourite number cost with **Enjoy!** Super tariff? _____

e) How much does calling your favourite number cost with Standard tariff? _____

How much will your texts and calls cost you?
Enjoy! Mobile Pay as you go tariffs

	Standard tariff 3 favourite numbers half price	**Extra tariff** When you top-up £12 a month	**Enjoy! Super tariff** ALL calls and texts
Calls (any UK mobile or standard fixed line numbers)	20p (per minute)	12p (per minute)	15p (per minute)
Text message (any UK mobile)	12p (per text)	6p (per text)	6p (per text)
	Your three favourite numbers		
Calls	10p (per minute)	–	–
Texts	6p (per text)	–	–

5 The statements below are about information in the table above. Put a cross by any statements that are false. Tick any statements that are true.

A Calls made to your favourite number on Standard tariff are more expensive than on **Enjoy!** Super tariff. ☐

B Texts made on Extra tariff are cheaper than on **Enjoy!** Super tariff. ☐

C Texts cost most on the Standard tariff. ☐

5 Understanding what an image adds to a text

First read this ...

If a text has an image you need to work out what information the image is giving you, especially if it is giving information that is not in the words.

1 Read the main text first. Ask yourself: *'What is it telling me?'*

2 Study every part of the image – headings, labels, the picture, words, arrows, etc. Ask yourself: *'What can I see? What does that tell me?'*

3 Compare the information in the image and the text. Ask yourself: *'What information does the image show that is not in the words? How does the image help me to understand the text?'*

Now try it!

1 Tick the statement below that best sums up what the pictures add to the instructions below.

A They show readers how an ink cartridge works. ☐

B They persuade readers to recycle their ink cartridges. ☐

C They show how difficult it is to recycle an ink cartridge. ☐

D They show how easy it is to recycle an ink cartridge. ☐

> These images show readers exactly how to send an old ink cartridge off to be recycled.

HP ink cartridge recycling instructions

Thank you for participating in the HP Planet partners HP Laser Jet and inkjet recycling programmes.
Please only send back original HP cartridges.
www.hp.com/recycle
Envelope is made from recyclable material.

© Hewlett-Packard Development Company, L.P

> The text thanks people for recycling their ink cartridge.

2 Study the images and text on each of the PC game covers below. Which PC game is most suitable for the following people? Put A, B, C or D in each of the boxes below.

A An adventurous 8-year-old.

B A girl who secretly wishes she could be a celebrity.

C An adult who quite enjoys feeling scared but hates bad language.

D A man who hates violence.

Meaning of symbols

 = game content suitable for people above this age

 = fear

 = bad language

 = violence

1

WAR ON MARS

Stranded on Mars, the crew of the spaceship Alana needs your help. Aliens from Mars are about to open fire on their ship. Can you rescue them and bring them safely back to Earth?

2

Star Maker

Will you be a famous actor, singer or musician? How will you cope with the pressure? Can you escape from the news hungry press?

3

Jungle March

Lost in the jungle – can you find your way out? You'll need to cut a path through the trees, find fresh water, decide what is safe to eat and deal with hungry snakes and tigers.

4

MI5 Spymaster

Can you uncover a plot by an unknown enemy? What if they plan to take over the world – do you have the skill and time to stop it happening?

Use the test below to find out how well you have mastered the skills in Section B.

These questions are all about the recipe opposite.

1   Which statement best sums up why the writer used subheadings?

A ☐ To make the text look better on the page.

B ☐ To help readers find the ingredients.

C ☐ To help readers find the method.

D ☐ To help readers find different pieces of information.

2   What do the bullet points in the first paragraph tell readers?

A ☐ How to make the pudding.

B ☐ What the pudding has in it.

C ☐ What the pudding is like and how to vary it.

D ☐ When to make the pudding.

3   Study the photograph. What information does it give that the text does not?

A ☐ It shows readers that they have to cook the pancakes.

B ☐ It shows readers how to toss the pancakes.

C ☐ It shows readers what a pancake tastes like.

D ☐ It tells readers they can just use shop-bought pancakes if they want.

4   What order are the numbered points in?

A ☐ Alphabetical order

B ☐ A random order

C ☐ The order in which they need to be carried out

D ☐ Order of size.

Check your answers.
How many did you get right? ☐ /4

Now fill your score in the chart on pages 94–95.

Chocolate and Pear Pancakes

- *Not only does this look* line 1
  impressive and taste delicious line 2
  – it's also easy to make. line 3

- *Try layering instead of rolling* line 4
  the pancakes and then you'll be line 5
  able to see the pear purée and line 6
  chocolate spread dripping down line 7
  over the stack of pancakes. line 8

- *For a dairy-free version replace* line 9
  the cow's milk with soya milk or line 10
  rice milk. line 11

Ingredients

125 g	plain flour	line 12
1	egg	line 13
250 ml	milk	line 14
	sunflower oil to cook	line 15
700 g	puréed pears	line 16
1 tsp	cinnamon (optional)	line 17
1 jar	chocolate spread	line 18

Method

1 Mix the flour and salt together. Make a well in the centre and break in the egg. line 19

2 Add half the milk and mix using a hand whisk. Then add the rest of the milk and line 20
whisk again until smooth. line 21

3 Heat a pancake pan or flat frying pan, add 1tbsp sunflower oil and coat the pan line 22
with the oil. Once the pan is hot, pour in enough batter to coat the base of the line 23
pan. line 24

4 Cook the pancake over a moderate heat. When the pancake is brown on one line 25
side flip it over and brown the other side. line 26

5 Turn the cooked pancake out onto a plate and spread with 1tbs chocolate line 27
spread, then spread 3tbs puréed pear (mixed with cinnamon if using). Roll up the line 28
pancake and place in a rectangular serving dish. line 29

6 Continue to cook and fill pancakes until all the batter is used up. line 30

7 Before serving, warm up any remaining chocolate spread and pour over the top line 31
of the row of rolled pancakes. line 32

C Understanding what writers want their readers to do

By the end of this section you will be more aware of what writers want their readers to do when they read a text. You will know how to:

▷ recognise that texts have different purposes: *instruct, describe, explain, persuade*

▷ understand different features in different types of text

▷ notice how writers use words in different types of text

▷ understand the use of formal or informal language.

You will then test out your mastery of these skills at the end of the section.

1 Recognising the purpose of a text

First read this ...

When you are asked to work out what job a text is doing:

■ read the whole text and ask yourself: *'What is it about?'* Sum it up in a sentence.

■ ask yourself: *'What is the text trying to do?'*

A text that tells or advises you about something is an **information** text.

E.g. Plain chocolate has more iron in it than milk chocolate.

A text that tells you how or why something works or happens is an **explanation**.

E.g. How chocolate is made. First the cocoa pods, which contain the cocoa beans, are harvested. Then the pods are crushed.

A text that tries to make you to want to do something is **persuasive**.

E.g. Try our fair trade chocolate – it's delicious!

A text that tells you how to do something is an **instruction**.

E.g. First melt the chocolate, then mix in the cornflakes.

A text that wants you to picture something is a **description**.

E.g. The melted chocolate shone like gloss paint.

Now try it!

1   Read each text below. Work out which kind of text it is. Draw a line to link it to the right text type in the box.

1 What is it about?
The youth club at Barmouth Youth Centre.

2 What is it trying to do?
Make readers want to go to the Kool Youth Club

A

KOOL YOUTH CLUB

Are you bored at weekends? Do you have nowhere to go? **COME AND BE KOOL AT BARMOUTH YOUTH CENTRE** Open 8 p.m.–10 p.m. on Friday, Saturday and Sunday nights.

- *Come* and enjoy the wide variety of activities which include: sport, games, drama, competitions, challenges, PS2 nights and computer games, trips and discos.
- *Come* and hang out with your mates.
- *Come* and make new friends.
- *Come* and be **Cool** at **Kool**!

B

In 1850 Levi Strauss bought lots of rolls of strong blue cloth and travelled to San Francisco where he hoped to make and sell tent and wagon covers to the huge number of people digging for gold. Unfortunately someone else had already had the same idea. He could not sell his cloth. Then he heard a miner complaining that his trousers kept getting ripped. Strauss decided to make really tough trousers out of his strong blue material. Soon all the miners wanted the Levi Strauss trousers, which became known as 'jeans'. Levi Strauss made a fortune.

C

When I opened the door of our flat I was surprised that the hallway looked so much lighter and brighter. At first I thought it was because all the clutter of football gear, shoes and junk had been cleared away and the floor had been mopped. But then I noticed the walls. Gone was the dingy blue and instead everywhere was pale cream.

Text types:
- information
- instruction
- description
- explanation
- persuasive

D

To barbecue kebabs

1   Make sure your kebab is on a metal skewer. A wooden one will catch fire.

2   Brush the kebab lightly with oil and place on the barbecue. Cook for about 20–30 minutes. Keep turning it regularly.

3   Test the meat is cooked by piercing it with a knife. If there is no pink meat and any juices run clear then it is cooked.

E

When you feel angry your body gets ready to fight. This is because adrenalin is released, which makes your heart beat faster and your liver work faster, which makes your temperature rise. At the same time your muscles tense because your brain is getting your muscles ready to fight. All this makes your body start to overheat so it tries to cool itself down, which is why you sweat more and go red in the face.

Instructions tell you **how to do something**. A writer uses particular words and features to help readers understand this.

- Sentences often start with a verb to tell you the action needed: *stir, chop, make*.

- Connectives are often used to link and sequence: *first, then, now, when, lastly*.

- Bullets are often used to list points, or numbers used to list points in the order you need to do them.

Now try it!

1 Use what you have just read to help you complete the labels describing the features of the instruction text below.

This text tells readers how to make _____.

Most of the sentences are commands (stir, bake) that begin with a _____.

These words are used to _____ _____ ideas.

These _____ tell you information in the order you need to follow it.

Flapjacks

Ingredients _____

    75 g butter or margarine
    50 g soft brown sugar
    30 ml golden syrup
    175 g rolled oats

Method _____

1 First pre-heat the oven to 180°C or Gas Mark 5. <u>Grease</u> an 18cm square tin.

2 Then <u>stir</u> the brown sugar and oats together in a heat-proof bowl.

3 Next **melt** the butter with the syrup in a saucepan over a low heat. Then **pour** it onto the oat mixture. **Stir** thoroughly.

4 **Turn** the mixture into the baking tin and **press down** well.

5 **Bake** for about 20 minutes until golden brown.

6 **Remove** from oven and leave for about 5 minutes. When it has cooled a little, **cut** into squares with a sharp knife and **loosen** slightly.

2 Below are four features of an instruction text. Find and
underline one example of each feature in the text below.
Then draw a line linking the feature to its example.

Features of instruction texts

A The text tells readers how
to do something.

B Most of the sentences are
commands that begin with
a verb.

C Sometimes words such as
first, *then*, *now*, *when*,
lastly are used to link and
sequence ideas.

D Information is given in
a list of bullet points or
numbered points.

Cats

Protect your pet when fireworks are around by
following our animal friendly firework code.

- Keep your cat indoors.
- Close all windows and curtains. Then switch on
music or television to drown out the noise.
- Leave your cat to take
refuge in a corner if
it wishes. Do not try
to tempt it out as this
could cause more
stress.
- Make sure your cat is
microchipped so that
it can be returned to
you if it escapes and
becomes lost.

3 Study the flapjack recipe and instructions about cats
again, and answer these questions.

a) Where is the list of ingredients placed in the recipe?

A At the beginning.

B In the middle.

C At the end.

D Beside the instructions.

b) What feature does the writer use in the recipe to make
it easy for the reader to follow the instructions in the
right order?

A Bold print.

B A title.

C Numbered points.

D Italics.

c) Why are the points in the text about cats given bullet
points rather than being numbered?

A The points have to be followed in the
order in which they are written.

B The points do not have to be followed
in any particular order.

First read this ...

Descriptions want readers to picture something. They often create an impression of what the thing is like by:

- appealing to the five senses: things you can see, hear, touch, taste, smell
- usually offering facts rather than opinions
- using adjectives (describing words): *red, old, tired, rough*
- sometimes making comparisons: *as red as the setting sun*.

A *fact* tells you information that you can check to see if it is true.
> *He had dyed his hair red.*

An *opinion* is just someone's point of view.
> *His hair looks really cool.*

Now try it!

1 Read the list of features below. Then draw a line to link each feature to an example and <u>underline</u> it in the text below.

Typical features of a description

a) Appeals to the five senses – tells you things you can see, hear, touch, taste or smell.

b) Offers facts rather than opinions.

c) Uses a lot of adjectives (describing words such as *red, old, tired, rough*).

Missing

Ash Patel

Aged 23, height 195 cm, medium build. Last seen at Birmingham Central Station on 31 September 2006 wearing dark blue jeans, new white trainers and a black sports top with a hood.

Ash had met up with friends in the shopping centre and was last seen buying a ticket at the station to travel home. Ash has to take medication regularly. His friends and family are very anxious to know that he is safe and well.

If you have any information please call 0800 123 1234 and leave a message.

Post Card

Dear Nissa

We're having a really cool time here! The beaches have beautiful white sand and the sea really is as blue as in the picture on the front of this postcard. The only thing I'm not enjoying is being woken up by noisy seagulls at 6.00 a.m. They sound worse than your brother's band! See you on Friday after we get back.

Love

Danielle

Miss Nissa Chandhri

18 Weavers Avenue

Cardiff

CF4 5HS

2 Now read the postcard above. Which senses does the writer appeal to in her description of the holiday?

_____

3 Circle three adjectives that describe the beach and the sea.

4 Find and <u>underline</u> a comparison the writer uses to describe the seagulls.

5 Think about the way the writer describes the holiday. She makes it sound:

A boring ☐   **B** unpleasant ☐

C a mixed experience ☐   **D** all good ☐

6 Read the news report and answer these questions.

a) <u>Underline</u> two adjectives that show you what the fire was like.

b) Circle one adjective that describes the feelings of the people involved.

7 The adjectives used in the news report make the fire seem:

A interesting ☐   **B** frightening ☐

C easy to deal with ☐   **D** annoying ☐

The fire started in the garage, which had some old petrol cans and paint in it. The blaze spread to the house and quickly reached the top floor. The [5] terrified family was woken by the thick smoke and overpowering heat but managed to climb out of the front bedroom window and jump down onto the lawn. [10] Worried neighbours called the fire brigade who arrived quickly but sadly the house is so badly damaged it will have to be demolished and rebuilt. [15]

4 Understanding explanation texts

⏸ First read this ...

Explanation texts tell readers how or why something works or happens. They often use:

- connecting words to show how or why something happens: *because, since, which, so, therefore, as a result, this means*

- sentences that contain chunks of meaning and show how parts of an explanation relate to each other, beginning with: *who, which, while,* or *because.*

▶▶ Now try it!

1   Draw a line linking each example highlighted in the text to the correct label. The first has been done for you.

1 The text tells you how or why something happens or how something works.

How to become a TV or film 'extra'

Extras are the people in the background who fill up scenes in advertisements, television programmes or films. Since they are needed to make a scene feel 'real', casting agents look for people of all ages, shapes and sizes. Therefore anyone can have the right 'look' to be chosen as an extra.

To stand a chance of being picked all you have to do is sign up with a good agency for extras, who will ask you to give them a CV and a photograph. Then you have to wait to be phoned if you are wanted.

Film and television production teams will then look at your details to see if you are right for their show. Casting agencies are not looking for exam results because what they want are people who will make their scene look right, who can get up early, are totally reliable and will get on and do the job.

2 Some of the sentences explaining why different kinds of people are needed as extras have these connectives in them: *because, since, which, so, therefore, as a result, this means.*

3 There are some sentences with chunks of meaning giving more detail about the main point that begin with the words: *who, which, when, while* or *because.*

2 Read the explanation below. Then tick any of the
underlined words and phrases that connect different ideas.

Using our online catalogue

When customers visit our website www.whatabargain.com they will be able to see
all our products and read the descriptions. When they decide to buy something all
they have to do is click on the button that says 'Buy' <u>so</u> the item is added to their
shopping basket. When someone has finished choosing then they <u>click on the 'ready
to pay'</u> icon <u>because</u> that makes them enter a secure area, <u>which means</u> no one can
steal their card number. Here they are asked to type in their payment card details.
At this stage they can still take things out of their basket but once they have paid for
something it is too late and <u>this means that</u> those items <u>will be sent to them</u>.

3 Read the memo below and study the underlined features that help
the writer to explain things effectively.

a) Which feature explains how to use the cards? Number: _____

b) Which feature explains *why* the cards are being given to staff? Number: _____

c) Study features 3, 4, and 5. The underlined words introduce
information about how cards will:

   A benefit staff   ☐

   B make life more complicated   ☐

   C save money   ☐

   D persuade staff to use the cards.   ☐

Memo

To: All Staff

When employees return their old identity card to the office on
Monday 21st October they will be photographed and issued
with a new swipe card with their name and a unique bar code
on it. The new cards, <u>which have been introduced to reduce
theft</u>, should be carried in your shirt pocket.
   <u>By pushing the card into the machine, which stands in the
security guard's room, and putting pound coins in the slot you
can 'charge up your card' ready to pay for your meals and
drinks</u>.
   <u>As a result</u> of this new system staff will be able to leave
their money safely locked away in the lockers in the security
guard's area. <u>This means that</u> no one has any reason to carry
money around the rest of the site, <u>which</u> should considerably
reduce the chance to lose things or have them stolen.

Bill Owen
Manager

1

2

3

4

5

First read this ...

A persuasive text tries to make the reader want to do something. Often, a persuasive text will:

- give reasons to make the reader want to do something

- give a lot of opinions – *a **beautiful** house: a **bargain at £35,000,000***

- appeal to readers' feelings – *Won't you save a poor starving orphan?*

- use different types of print to make ideas stand out, e.g. **bold**, colour, CAPITALS, *italics*.

> A *fact* tells you information that you can check to see if it is true.
> *The house was bought for £35,000,000.*

> An *opinion* is just someone's point of view.
> *That's an outrageous amount to pay for a house!*

Now try it!

1   Read this appeal from a charity and work out how the writer has persuaded readers.

a) Tick the statement that best describes what the writer wants the reader to do.

A   To think carefully before buying a dog. ☐

B   To give money to the charity that looks after dogs. ☐

C   To adopt one of the charity's dogs. ☐

D   To buy a dog from the charity. ☐

b) Study the underlined words in the text below. They are reasons the writer gives to make the reader want to do something. Find and underline two more.

c) Are any opinions given in the text that tell you how the dog or charity views sponsors?

Yes ☐   No ☐

Put a star by any you find.

d) Circle any of the feelings in the box below that you think the text tries to appeal to.

| pride | pity | greed | love |
| sadness | anger | kindness |
| jealousy |

So much love to give.
So little to ask.

£1 a week means a huge amount to an abandoned dog like me. Your gift will help Dog's Trust give us all the love and support we need. They will never put a healthy dog down and your pound means that they can take care of us – for ever. When you become a sponsor, we'll send you photos and news of what we have been up to. Could you spare as little as £1 a week? You'd receive so much love in return.

SPONSOR A DOG FOR £1 A WEEK AND YOU'LL HAVE A FRIEND FOR LIFE.

e) Read the different types of print listed in the box below. Circle the ones that are used to make words stand out in the advertisement on page 40.

bold	colour	CAPITALS	*italics*

2 Study the advertisement below. Work out how it persuades readers by doing the activities below.

a) Complete this sentence:

This text is trying to make readers want to

_____ .

b) Study the underlined words in the text. They are reasons the writer gives to make the reader want to do something. Find and underline two more.

AS THE ULTIMATE retail and leisure resort in Littleton, *Blue Horizons Shopping and Leisure* provides a great atmosphere for the whole family, during both the day and the evening.

Come and visit us for retail therapy, to eat out, or to enjoy our leisure facilities at the *Horizons Leisure Centre.*

Everything is on one level, with plenty of parking spaces and easy wheelchair access.

So if you're looking for that *little black dress* for a night out on the town, some casual clothes for a day on the golf course, or a romantic meal out for two, *Blue Horizons* has it all under one roof.

There are several restaurants to tickle your taste buds, from burgers to the best of Chinese and Italian cuisine.

If you've overindulged, pop into the *Leisure Centre.* We have a fantastic gym with up to the minute equipment, or if you just want to chill out after a hard day at work, why not try our Spa and pool complex? 20

If you fancy a family night out together, try our *multiplex cinema,* which shows all the latest movies.

BLUE HORIZONS SHOPPING AND LEISURE 25
The Hill, Littleton, Hants SP10 9HN
Tel: 01548 888444
Website: www.bluehorizons.co.net

c) The writer includes lots of opinions in this text that make visiting Blue Horizons Shopping and Leisure sound attractive. Find and put a star by four of them.

d) Circle any of the feelings in the box below that you think the text tries to appeal to.

pride	pity	greed	love	sadness
	anger	kindness	enjoyment	

e) Read the different types of print listed in the box below. Circle the ones that are used to make words stand out in the advertisement.

bold	colour	CAPITALS	*italics*

6 Formal and informal texts

First read this ...

Texts can be **informal** (such as letters to friends) or **formal** (such as business letters). When you are writing a *formal text* you need to make sure that all your sentences are written in formal English. You should:

- use the proper name for things: *jewellery* not *bling*

- write in complete words: *going to* not *gonna; and* not *&; information* not *info*

- not use text messaging: *Are you okay?* not *RUOK? To/too/two* not *2; later* not *l8er*

- not use any slang: *cool, cheers, mate*

- not use abbreviations: *could've, wouldn't, can't, won't.*

Now try it!

1 The text below has a space. <u>Underline</u> the phrase in the box underneath that is too informal to use in the space.

> *Treasure Chest* hereby _____ that £1,500,000 has been placed on deposit with BG Bank plc, Liverpool, to cover the prizes offered in the Win a Million Prize Draw. Treasure Chest guarantees all the prizes in this prize draw.
>
> Signed: *N.O. Bling*

| declares | gives the info | informs readers | promises |

2 Read the hotel notice below. It is meant to be formal. <u>Underline</u> any words in it that are not formal enough.

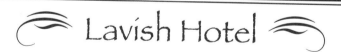

> ≈ Lavish Hotel ≈
>
> Guests are kindly requested not to smoke in any of the bedrooms or public areas. There is a designated smoking room available on the ground floor. So if you wanna smell of fags – go find it! Please ask at reception for further info.

3 The underlined words in this insurance claim form are too informal. Write a more formal alternative above the underlined words.

> I had offered to drive my <u>mate</u> to her home in Westby because <u>she'd</u> run out of cash. It had been <u>chucking it down</u> earlier in the day <u>&</u> there was a lot of water on the road's surface. Therefore I <u>was goin'</u> well under 90 mph.
>
> 5   I had just reached the motorway junction when I saw a police car with a blue flashing light following me so I applied my brakes. But I <u>couldn't</u> control the car. That was when my car went <u>kinda skiddin'</u> out of control, bounced into the hard shoulder, spun right round and <u>b4</u>
>
> 10   I could stop, hit the police car.

4 Find the five abbreviated words in this news report. Circle each abbreviation and then write out the full version of the words above it.

> There has been a flash flood in Norton. It's been raining heavily all night with the result that there's a flood in the Lower Street area. People there have been told to leave their homes but many aren't going. They
>
> 5   won't leave behind pets or valuables. The emergency services expect to work thro' the night.

5 This e-mail is meant to be very informal. <u>Underline</u> any phrases that you think sound too formal and write a more informal phrase above each one.

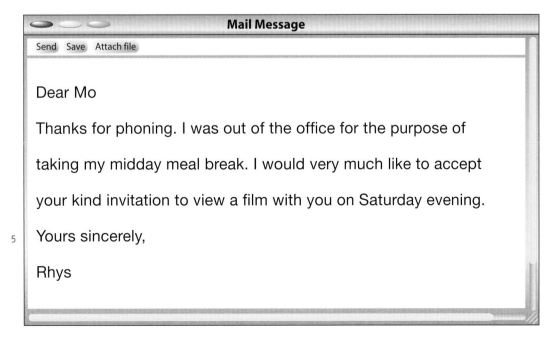

Mail Message

Send   Save   Attach file

Dear Mo

Thanks for phoning. I was out of the office for the purpose of taking my midday meal break. I would very much like to accept your kind invitation to view a film with you on Saturday evening.

5   Yours sincerely,

Rhys

Choosing to be formal

When you write a text you have to decide how formal you want to sound. You should:

■ be very formal when you are writing to people you do not know at all

■ be formal when you write to someone because of their job (even if you have met)

■ only write informally to friends or members of your family.

Now try it!

1   Decide whether you should use formal English (F) or informal English (I) in the situations below. Write *F* or *I*.

   a) You are writing to a relative or close friend.   _____

   b) You are writing a **business** letter, e-mail or report. _____

   c) You are writing a **personal** letter, postcard, e-mail or text message.   _____

   d) You are writing to someone because of the job or responsibility they have.   _____

2   Use the chart below to help you choose a suitable greeting or ending to write in the gap on each of the letters being sent to Jade Stone on page 45.

How formal	Begin a letter with:	Sign off with:
Formal	Dear Sir or Madam	Yours faithfully
Formal	Dear Mr, Mrs or Ms Stone	Yours sincerely
Less formal	Dear Jade Stone	Yours sincerely/ Yours truly/Best wishes/Kind regards
Informal	Dear Jade	Much love/Love/ Cheers

3   Read each statement below and note whether it is formal (F) or informal (I). Write *F* or *I*.

   a) According to the instructions the batteries should have been included.   _____

   b) He trashed his bedroom.   _____

   c) You won't C me till Thurs   _____

   d) I look forward to hearing from you.   _____

4 It is important to keep the same level of formality all the way through a text. Read the letters below.

a) Decide which are formal (F) and which are informal (I) and note this by ticking the relevant box.

b) Underline any sentences that are too informal when they should be formal.

A

Dear _____

Thanks for inviting me to your wedding. I'm really looking forward to sharing your special day. Do let me have a copy of your present list won't you?

Much love

Mariam

F ☐   I ☐

B

The Best Hotel
Allswell
ME4 UCW
13 November 2006

Ms J Stone
1 Borem Lane
Allswell
EM1 2XX

Dear Ms Stone

I have great pleasure in confirming your booking for your wedding reception to be held on 29 April 2007 at 12.30 p.m. I'm sure it'll be a fab day. Our catering manager will be in contact with you shortly to discuss your requirements.

_____

Tasneem Khan

Bookings Manager

F ☐   I ☐

C

Love Me Do
High Street
Cheetam
YME 7TR

Ms Jade Stone
1 Borem Lane
Allswell
EM1 2XX

Dear _____

Please note that Love Me Do is no longer able to offer the 'Complete Bride Package' as advertised in The Cheetam Express. They have gone bust. I enclose your cheque.

_____

Nigel Pennypincher

Nigel Pennypincher
Chief Accountant

F ☐   I ☐

First read this ...

Use the test below to find out how well you have mastered the skills in Section C.

These questions are all about the text opposite.

1   The purpose of the document is:

A ☐   to inform

B ☐   to describe

C ☐   to persuade

D ☐   to explain.

2   Which is the best explanation of why the writer of the text has written the words VOLKSWAGEN GOLF and CASH in large, red capital letters?

A ☐   To make those words stand out.

B ☐   To match the red colour of the car.

C ☐   To make the page look more interesting.

D ☐   To make readers want to win them.

3   Which word in lines 18–21 is informal?

A ☐   affix

B ☐   represents

C ☐   cash

D ☐   provided.

4   Which of these lines in the text has a sentence that is not persuasive?

A ☐   lines 1–4

B ☐   line 5

C ☐   lines 12–16

D ☐   lines 19–21.

> Check your answers.
> How many did you get right?   ☐ /4

Now fill your score in the chart on pages 94–95.

You could soon drive away in this
line 1

VOLKSWAGEN GOLF or take £18,000
line 2

CASH!
line 3

SPECIAL PRIZE ON RESERVE! MAKE YOUR CHOICE <u>NOW</u>!
line 4

When you say YES to Reader's
line 5
Digest, as a special thank you, we'll
line 6
guarantee your opportunity to win the
line 7
£18,000 Special Prize of your choice
line 8
in a subscriber-only Contest.
line 9

But you have to act fast! We must
line 10
have your reply within seven days
line 11
of receipt. Tell us now which prize
line 12
you would prefer, the luxurious
line 13
Volkswagen Golf 2.0 FSI GT
line 14
hatchback pictured above,
line 15
or £18,000 in CASH!
line 16

Once you have decided, remove the
line 17
SPECIAL PRIZE label that represents
line 18
your choice of CAR or CASH and
line 19
affix it to your YES reply envelope
line 20
in the space provided. Then be sure
line 21
to return it within the seven-day
line 22
deadline.
line 23

DON'T MISS OUT –
line 24
REPLY WITHIN SEVEN
line 25
DAYS!
line 26

D Spelling words correctly

By the end of this section you should have improved your spelling by:

▷▷ using spelling strategies

▷▷ learning spellings: *most-used words; words with the same letter patterns; words that sound the same but are spelt differently*

▷▷ spotting when words are wrongly spelt.

You will then test out your mastery of these skills at the end of the section.

1 Learning to spell commonly used words

First read this ...

The best way to become a good speller is to learn how to spell words you often get wrong, rather than hope that somehow you will spell them right this time.

- **Look** carefully at the word.
  - a Sound out each part of the word (e.g. *d-i-ff-e-r-e-n-t*)
  - b Break it up into syllables (e.g. *dif-fer-ent*)
  - c Spot the part that is tricky (e.g. *diff**er**ent*)
    (The tricky part might be a silent letter, e.g. <u>k</u>now; double letters, e.g. nece<u>ss</u>ary; the vowels, e.g. bec<u>au</u>se; or how to add an ending such as -ly, e.g. quick<u>ly</u>.)

- **Say** the word to yourself, spelling it out several times.

- **Cover** the word when you think you know how to spell it.

- **Write** the word out from memory. Does it look right?

- **Check** to see if you spelt it right.
  Yes – Well done!
  No – Follow the same steps again until you can.

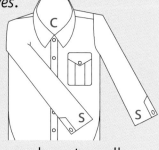

▶▶ Now try it!

1   Below are seven words that people often find difficult.
Practise the five steps and learn to spell each one, or try
it with words that you find difficult. Fold the page back to
cover the word and test yourself on each from memory.

Fold

Word	Tricky part
1 because	_because_
2 which	
3 until	
4 knew	
5 friend	
6 sight	
7 separate	

Test yourself	
	☐
	☐
	☐
	☐
	☐
	☐
	☐

2   In the table below list five words that you have trouble
spelling. Then follow the five steps and learn to spell
them.

Word	Tricky part
1	
2	
3	
4	
5	

Test yourself	
	☐
	☐
	☐
	☐
	☐

3   How quickly can you learn to spell the words below? If you
don't find these spellings difficult, choose words that you
do have trouble spelling.

Word	Tricky part	Memory Aid	Test yourself	
1 necessary				☐
2 Wednesday				☐
3 February				☐
4 receive				☐
5 unusual				☐
6 sincerely				☐
7 different				☐

2 Spelling words with common letter patterns correctly

Many words share the same letter patterns, e.g. b**old**, c**old**, f**old**, g**old**, h**old**. Knowing which words share a pattern helps you learn to spell more words and spot when a word is wrongly spelt.

■ **Learn** some common letter patterns and the words that share them.

■ **Use** what you know to spell correctly and to spot spelling mistakes.

▶▶ Now try it!

1　Study each of the spelling patterns in the table below.

　a) Underline words in the example column that share the same pattern.

　b) Add more words with the same pattern to the third column.

　c) Notice any rules for this spelling pattern. There may be exceptions to the rule, but it is a useful rule to remember.

Spelling pattern	Underline the examples	Add more examples	Match up these parts of words to help you add examples.
-ie	Much to the relief of the thief, the Chief of Police came to grief while chasing him.	_____ _____ *Rule: i before e except after c.*	ach bel　　**ie**　　ve rel
-ei	I want to receive a receipt for payment of eight pounds.	_____ _____ _____ _____ *Rule: e before i when the ei comes after c, or the vowel sound does <u>not</u> rhyme with see.*	v　　　　　l w　　　　　rd w　　**ei**　ght c h　　　　ling
-ough	The horse pulling the plough through rough grass has a cough.	_____ _____ _____ _____ _____ _____ *Did you notice that the same letters can have a different sound in different words?*	alth d 　　**ough** en r　　　　　ly
-ll-	Rick was cancelling the marvellous holiday because he didn't like travelling.	_____ _____ _____ _____ _____ _____ *Rule: after a single vowel, the l is doubled.*	ca　　　　ed fi　　**ll**　ing te　　　　ious rebe

Spelling pattern	Underline the examples	Add more examples	Match up these parts of words to help you add examples.		
qu-	Quickly and quietly he picked up the quivering arrow that had missed the Queen.	_____ _____ _____ _____ _____ _____	**qu**	i e	te et ck z stion
Silent g-	The gnat was gnawing on the sign.	_____ _____ _____ _____ _____	desi resi alig	**g**	n nome narled
Silent k-	He knew the knight was kneeling down.	_____ _____ _____ _____ _____ _____ *If you sound out the 'k' as you spell the word, it will help you remember how to spell it.*	**k**		nob nit nife not nock now
Silent -gh-	He sighed because the bright light was slightly too high.	_____ _____ _____ _____ _____ _____	mi ou nou nau si	**gh**	t tful ty ing ly

2 Choose the correct letter pattern from the box to complete the words in the passage below.

ie	ei	ough
ll	qu	g
k	gh	

Tough cop Rock Adam rec___ves a mysterious mobile phone call just before he begins his late shift. The ca___er warns him to stay in toni___t if he wants to avoid
5 b___ng cau___t and injured in a major gang fi__t. Rock bel___ves the ca___er is his wife – but she's been dead for five years, or has she?
Tracing the mobile call to a bi___iard hall in
10 a r_____n_____bourhood, Rock __nocks on doors to ask lots of __ __estions. He starts his en__ir__ __s and soon discovers everyone is afraid of the _____t barman at the billiard hall. Even the Ch___f of Police seems to be dec___ving Rock as the plot twists and turns, keeping you guessing ri___t up to the end.

Unmissable ★★★★

51

3 Practising spotting spelling mistakes

When you have written a text or are asked to proofread one you need to try and spot any spelling mistakes. Follow these steps:

5 Should any word have **double letters**? (e.g. *borrowing*.)

4 Does this word belong to a **word family** you know? Does it follow the same pattern? (e.g. *right, sight, light, might*.)

3 Sound out the word (e.g. *l-i-b-r-a-r-y*). Are all the sounds there?

2 Break the word up into syllables (e.g. *li-brar-y*). Are all the syllables there?

1 Read each sentence slowly word by word. Do any words look wrong? Work on these words. (You might even find they are spelt right anyway!) Underline them if you can.
I might be borowing a book from the libary.

Now try it!

1 Circle the one word that is wrongly spelt in each of these sentences. Use a dictionary to check the right spelling. Write it below at the end of each sentence and learn it. The first one has been done for you. Then in the box of common errors below, note which type of error each is by adding the letter.

a) My friend is a CCTV operator in a goverment building.   *government*

b) The CCTV cameras had tapped a crime taking place.   _____

c) A hooded thief took a large amout of computer hardware.   _____

d) On three ocasions the hooded thief was filmed at the back door.   _____

e) In a seprate shot, the thief was caught with his hood down.   _____

f) It was not neccesary to start a search.   _____

g) The thief was defanately a man who lived down the street.   _____

Common errors	Letter
missing letters	a)
incorrect letter	_____
a single letter where there should be double letters	_____
double letters where there should be a single letter	_____

2 Which word is wrongly spelt in this paragraph?

> She was very unusul looking. One eye was hazel, the other was light blue and the third was green.

A unusul ☐   **B** hazel ☐
C light ☐   **D** blue ☐

3 Which of the spellings below should be used to fill in the blank in this sentence?

> Letters of application should be sent to the _____ at the bottom of this advertisement.

A address ☐   **B** adress ☐
C addres ☐   **D** adres ☐

4 Circle the word below that is spelt incorrectly.

> I am intrested in applying for the position.

5 Underline the word that is spelt incorrectly in the first sentence of this paragraph.

> When you use a ladder outside make sure it is resting on a flat surfise. Stand it on a plank if the ground is soft. It is very difficult to stay safe on a wobbly ladder.

6 Which of the words below should be used to fill the gap in the first sentence?

> To _____ the best results make sure you stir the mixture thoroughly. Do not begin spreading the paste on the wallpaper until all the lumps have disappeared.

A acheeve ☐   **B** achieve ☐
C acheive ☐   **D** acheave ☐

7 Circle the word that is spelt incorrectly in this passage.

> Fire officers checked the burnt out building thoroghly but there was no sign of the missing tiger. The pet may well have escaped before the garage was burnt.

8 Which of the words below should be used instead of the underlined word in the first sentence?

> Tom was looking forward to weering his new football boots. With them he was less likely to slip over on the muddy pitch and more likely to score a goal.

A wering ☐   **B** weiring ☐
C wiering ☐   **D** wearing ☐

Spotting words that sound the same but are spelt differently

People often mix up words that sound the same but are spelt differently, e.g. *their, there* and *they're*. A good way to try to avoid making this mistake is to:

■ work out what the different spellings of the word mean

■ work out which meaning makes sense in the sentence.

▶▶ *Now try it!*

1   Work out what the different spellings of the word mean. Add another example of the word being used correctly to this chart.

Word	What it means	Example	Your example
to	part of the action/verb	One day I want **to** run the London Marathon.	
to	shows where someone went	He went **to** Liverpool on the ferry.	
too	also or as well	If she's going to the party, I want to go **too**.	
too	a lot or more than reasonable	Was eating fourteen cream cakes **too** greedy?	
two	number 2	My **two** dogs are a pitbull called Peace and a poodle called Jaws.	

2   Which *to/too/two* is needed in each of these sentences? Write in the right word.

a) I want _____ have a barbecue this evening.

b) We will need to cook at least _____ packets of burgers for everyone.

c) If you go _____ Savalot they are selling _____ for the price of one so you will save _____ pounds.

d) We could get _____ packages of sausages _____ cook, _____.

e) I just want _____ check if my team-mates can come _____.

f) Do you think starting at 8.00 p.m. is _____ late?

3 Circle five wrong uses of *to/too/two* in the passage below. Write the correct spellings above the wrong words.

> Lee went two Savalot too buy the sausages. They were offering two for the price of one. He couldn't decide if to packets would be two much. He phoned his friend to check. She said he needed too buy four packets not two.

4 The words *there/their/they're* all sound the same but have different meanings. Answer the questions below, using *there/their/they're*.

a) When we got _____ all the food was cooked already.

b) I was so pleased to see _____ was a chocolate fudge brownie pudding too.

c) _____ friends are really nice people.

d) _____ going to ask me to do some babysitting for them.

e) Lee said _____ garden was too small for all _____ friends to fit in.

Remember

■ **There** is a place, e.g. *The referee is standing over there*.
■ **There** goes with the verb 'to be', e.g. *There are two players with him*.
■ **Their** means belonging to them, e.g. *He's taking a note of their names*.
■ **They're** is short for 'they are', e.g. *They're going to be in a lot of trouble*.

5 Find five wrong uses of *there/their/they're* in this text, and circle them.

> I like going to their house because most of they're friends are really chatty. I feel a bit shy with people if their a bit quiet too. Lee's friends are really into dancing. They're always jumping up when he puts there favourite music on. Their are a couple of really nice girls who always get my mum and auntie up on they're feet too.

6 In the text below are words that sound the same but are spelt differently. Circle the right word that should be used each time.

> I could have stayed longer but there/their/they're was the morning to think about. I had to be up early and get down to/too/two the shop by seven or I would be to/too/two late to/too/two start work. Lee said the last people left at to/too/two o'clock but there/their/they're was a lot of clearing up to do. He thought it was great, except for having to clear up.

5 Spelling what you mean

First read this ...

Sometimes words are similar but spelt differently, and you have to decide which spelling is right for the word you need.

Jot down the different ways of spelling the word and what each means.

■ Ask yourself: *'Which word will make sense in this sentence?'*

Choice of spellings	What each spelling means	Which spelling makes sense in this sentence? *He could___ asked me to go to the cinema.*
've	've is short for have	He could've asked me to go to the cinema. ✓
of	= belonging to = about	He could of asked me to go to the cinema. ☒ **Never** write *should of, could of, would of, might of* etc.

Now try it!

1   Use the tables below to help you decide which words are needed in the sentences below. Circle the word that is right.

Choice of spelling	What each spelling means
of	belonging to, or about
off	the opposite of on
've	short for have

a) Turn of/off the tap when you brush your teeth!

b) In one day you will 've/of saved a lot of water.

Choice of spelling	What spelling means
accept	allow or receive
except	not this one not allowed

c) Shop with us! We accept/except all major credit cards.

d) You can use all major credit cards accept/except for American Express.

2 Find the 13 mistakes in the draft advertisement below.
Note each mistake and the correct spelling underneath.

A brand knew shopping centre is opening and looking for staff

Wanted: reliable, hardworking, enthusiastic people to become:

Knight security officer

you will need to where full uniform at all times.

Flour seller

if your used to making up bouquets quickly and have a good I for colour, get in touch.

Hair stylists

we're looking for two stylists with bald new ideas. Successful candidates must of passed relevant qualifications and be able to show there certificates.

Electrician

currant position – must be willing to except a 6 month contract but may become permanent.

Interested? Right for application forms two:
Dawn Dowter at Jobs4U, Hope Way, Gonnerby, DE1 2ZR

	Mistake	Correct spelling
1		
2		
3		
4		
5		
6		
7		
8		
9		
10		
11		
12		
13		

Use the test below to find out how well you have mastered the skills in Section D.

Read the letter opposite and answer the questions below.

1   Which of these lines has a spelling mistake in it?

A ☐ line 9

B ☐ line 10

C ☐ line 12

D ☐ line 25

2   How should the word underlined on line 17 be spelt?

A ☐ furnature

B ☐ ferniture

C ☐ furniture

D ☐ furnatiour

3   Which of the words below should be used to fill in the blank on line 20?

A ☐ to

B ☐ too

C ☐ two

D ☐ tow

4   Which of these words should be used to fill in the blank on line 22?

A ☐ there

B ☐ their

C ☐ theyr

D ☐ they're

5   Which of the words below is spelt wrongly?

A ☐ Saturday on line 11

B ☐ singel on line 15

C ☐ available on line 19

D ☐ Wednesday on line 24

6 Which word is wrongly spelt on line 23?

A ☐ through

B ☐ temperatures

C ☐ reached

D ☐ there

Check your answers.
How many did you get right? ☐ /6

48

Now fill your score in the chart on pages 94–95.

86 Weir Street	line 1
Wissely	line 2
OHN 0ZY	line 3
12 August 2006	line 4
	line 5
FABHOLS	line 6
274 High Street	line 7
Bellmont	line 8
BR16 7NX	line 9
Dear Sir or Madam	
I wish to complain about the holyday I went on with your	line 10
company. We arrived at 10 p.m. on Saturday to discover that	line 11
the Belle Vista Hotel was full and that their computer was down.	line 12
They said there were no family rooms left and that they had no	line 13
record of our booking. My wife and our four children ended up	line 14
spending the night crammed into a singel bedroom sleeping on a	line 15
row of three bunk beds pushed together. It was so crowded that	line 16
no other <u>furnature</u> could fit in the room. The following morning	line 17
the computer was working and our booking was confirmed – but	line 18
there were no other rooms available. The other local hotels were	line 19
all full up _____. Your rep said their was nothing he	line 20
could do and there were no flights home till the next Saturday.	line 21
We had no choice but to stay _____ for the rest of the	line 22
week even through the temperatures reached 100 and there was	line 23
no air conditioning. On the Wednesday the shower blocked up	line 24
and flooded so all our suitcases storing our clothes got soaked.	line 25
I would like a full refund and £10,000 compensation.	line 26
Yours faithfully	line 27

Ewan Geddit

Ewan Geddit

E Using punctuation correctly

By the end of this section you will understand how punctuation helps to make your meaning clear in sentences. You will learn how to:

➤➤ use capital letters, full stops, exclamation marks and question marks

➤➤ write complete sentences

➤➤ write in paragraphs.

1 Capital letters

❚❚ First read this ...

You need to know when to use a capital letter in your own writing. You also need to be able to spot when one has been missed out or wrongly used in a text.

There are two main uses for capital letters:

■ A capital letter begins every sentence.

■ A capital letter begins certain important words, such as people's names and places.

➤➤ Now try it!

1 This table lists the uses of a capital letter. It gives examples of each of the different uses. Add your own example of each use in the third column.

Use a capital letter to begin ...	Example	Add your example
the first word of a sentence	*Today it will be dry.*	
the days of the week, months, occasions	*Wednesday July* *Diwali*	
the words in someone's name	*Robbie Williams* *Raj Sharma*	
the title and initials in a name	*Mr B. J. Harris Dr F. Robson*	
the pronoun I	*Do you think I am wrong?*	
the main words in a place, organisation or event	*Birmingham* *Bradford on Avon* *Bartholomew School* *Glastonbury Festival*	
the main words in the titles of books, films, TV programmes, etc.	*Big Brother* *The Da Vinci Code* *The Bumper Book of Jokes*	

2 Some of the capital letters in the magazine extract below have been highlighted in blue. Draw lines to match each one with one of the labels explaining why a capital letter is needed.

The pronoun I should always be a capital letter.

Begin the title of a show or event with a capital letter.

Begin the name of a particular person, place or organisation with a capital letter.

Begin the days of the week, months and special occasions with a capital letter.

The party season is nearly here, but are you and your mates going to be ready?
Win the chance to take part in **R**eally Cool Yule, our brilliant party makeover event. You'll have a fab time – **I** promise! You'll be pampered by top hairdresser **T**rim **Z** **F**ringe, make-up artist **T** **J** and stylist **W**anda **F**rill, and just 'cos it's **C**hristmas you even get to keep your outfits!
Just fill in the blurb below telling us why you deserve to win and pop it in the post. Entries must be received by **N**ovember 21st.

Initials should always be in capital letters.

3 Proof-read the memo below. Circle the nine letters that should be capital letters.

Memo

To: All staff

From: toby childs

Subject: More reader involvement

we need to get more readers on the pages of *allstars magazine*. The Deputy Editor wants readers to send in their 'Have Your say' answers together with a photograph to win the chance to interview David Beckham for the BBC. That project will be handled by Greta fann. she will present the details of how it will work at tuesday's meeting.

4 You are Today's Star Reader. Fill in the gaps in the article on the right, making sure you use capital letters correctly.

★ ★ ★ ★ ★ ★ ★ ★ ★ ★ ★ ★

Today's Star Reader is

_____.

Two celebrities I'd like to meet are

_____

_____

Two places I'd like to visit are

_____

_____

My favourite magazine is

_____

A TV show I'd like to appear on is

_____

My best day out would be going to

_____

The best advice I've been given is

_____

_____

First read this ...

A sentence is a group of words that make complete sense together.
For example, here is a sentence: '*I went to the football match.*'
This is not a sentence: '*I went to.*'

Most sentences end with a full stop. Some sentences end with a
question mark (?) or an exclamation mark (!).

You need to know when to use these three punctuation marks. You
also need to be able to spot when they have been missed out or
used wrongly.

Now try it!

1   Most sentences are **statements**. They end with a full stop:

■ *We were winning 3–2 at half time.*

■ *I'll see you on Tuesday.*

Some sentences are **questions**. They end with a question mark.
Read and complete the chart below with your own examples.

How to write a question	Example	Your examples
Questions often begin with a question word, such as **who**, **what**, **when**, **where**, **which**, **why**, **how**.	*Which games show would you like to go on?* *Who will you choose for 'phone a friend'?* *How much money do you think you will win?*	
Sometimes questions start with a different word, but they still demand an answer.	*Are you going to ask Victoria?* *Does she know much about sport?* *Have you got anyone else in mind?*	

2   Add a full stop or a question mark to the sentences below, so
    that they make sense.

   a) Which English captain stood down after the 2006 World Cup

   b) Can I phone a friend

   c) I think it was Wayne Rooney

   d) Is that your final answer

   e) What do you think you will do with your £100 prize

3 Some sentences 'shout' at you. They could be commands or exclamations. This type of sentence ends in an exclamation mark:

■ *Take it away right now!*

■ *It'll be a fab party!*

Read the job advertisement below. Put a full stop, a question mark or an exclamation mark at the end of each sentence.

Are you looking for a decorator who is hard working and experienced

Do you want your home left clean and tidy

Look no further

Call Mark Walls on 324774

References are available

Decorators

4 Read this e-mail and answer the question below.

Mail Message	
Send Save Attach file	
Hi Winston	line 1
How are you?	line 2
I've been checking out Country Farm Campsite. It's about 30 km in from	line 3
the coast, and looks very comfy. Jardine would love seeing the lambs	line 4
and piglets – she's so crazy about animals? The farm has a shop that	line 5
sells fresh bread and milk.	line 6
On the down side, the beach is nearly an hour away. Are we really	line 7
going to want to do that drive every day. And I may get fed up with	line 8
cockerels crowing at 5.00 a.m. every morning too!	line 9
Perhaps we should go to Clifftop Campsite instead. What do you think?	line 10
Ellie x	line 11

The writer of this e-mail has not ended her sentences properly in two places. Which are they?

A lines 2 and 9 ☐   **B** lines 3 and 5 ☐

C lines 5 and 8 ☐   **D** lines 6 and 8 ☐

First read this ...

Using sentences helps your reader to understand your ideas.
A sentence has to:

■ make sense on its own, e.g.
We are going to the Bexham Festival. ✓
Bexham Festival in August ✗

■ have a verb (an action word or phrase), e.g. *He plays the guitar.* Or *My favourite band, Cold Heart, will be playing.*

■ begin with a capital letter and end with a full stop, question mark or exclamation mark (see pages 60–63).

▶▶ Now try it!

1 Put a tick against the correct sentences below, and a cross against the sentences that are not complete.

a) Welcome to the Computer Warehouse.

b) Our July Buyers' Guide.

c) As you'd expect, we have the widest range of computers in the UK.

d) Your shopping easy.

e) We have some fantastic new savings this summer.

2 Some sentences consist of two statements linked together:

| We are going on holiday this summer, | and | we are really looking forward to it. |

Statement 1   Joining word   Statement 2

Connectives (joining words) often used to link the two ideas are: *and*, *but*, *or*. Sometimes there is a comma before the connective.

Each sentence in the advertisement on the right has two main parts linked by a connective. Find and <u>underline</u> each of the connectives.

Castlehill is a well-organised site and it has wonderful views over the cove. The site has three shops and a restaurant, and boasts a heated outdoor swimming pool. The coast is easily accessible, but elderly visitors may find the steps to the cove challenging.

3   You need to know when to use a comma and when to use a full stop in a sentence. Read the pairs of sentences below. Tick the line that is punctuated correctly.

a) ☐ The night life is good, there are lots of discos.
    ☐ The night life is good. There are lots of discos.

b) ☐ There is a shop on site, but it is probably expensive.
    ☐ There is a shop on site. But it is probably expensive.

c) ☐ We could rent a caravan, it is probably cheaper.
    ☐ We could rent a caravan. It is probably cheaper.

Read this newspaper extract and answer Questions 4 and 5.

Lifeboat crew are trained for anything but, no one could have predicted   line 1
the high drama that took place at Invergordon on 15 January.   line 2
  Following a mayday call from the cargo ship East Wind, the lifeboat   line 3
was launched at 7.45 p.m. The lifeboat stood by until 11 p.m., ready to   line 4
offer assistance, but then two of the ship's crew were spotted jumping   line 5
into the water and swimming desperately towards the rocks.   line 6

4   Line 1 of the news article needs punctuating correctly. The correct punctuation should be:

A for anything, but no one could   ☐
B for anything. But, no one could   ☐
C for anything but. No one could   ☐
D for anything but no one, could   ☐

5   Lines 4–6 of the news article could be improved by splitting them into two shorter sentences. What word needs to be removed before adding a full stop?

A then   ☐
B but   ☐
C and   ☐
D were   ☐

Starting a new paragraph

First read this ...

When you are writing a longer text it needs to be organised in paragraphs. A paragraph is a group of sentences about the same topic or subject. You need to start a new paragraph when you begin writing about a new:

- person
- place
- time
- event
- idea.

Test tip

In the test you may be asked to break a long paragraph into two. You need to be able to spot:

- the sentence where one idea ends
- the next sentence where a different idea begins.

You may also be asked why a new paragraph has been started at a particular place. Usually, the new paragraph was needed because the writer began to write about a new person, place, time event or idea.

Now try it!

1 Read the report on the right. Then complete the sentences below. The first one has been done for you.

Report on Charity Fundraising Party

The party will be held on July	line 1
7th 2007 in the Events Room at	line 2
the Nightingale Sports Centre on	line 3
Darkling Road, Hampstead. It will	line 4
have a James Bond theme. Tickets	line 5
will go on sale in March and will	line 6
cost £30, to include food but not	line 7
drinks. The bar will be open all	line 8
evening. The last party raised over	line 9
£5000 for Cancer Research and had	line 10
a Wild West theme. It was held at	line 11
Atkins Farm.	line 12

a) The first four sentences are about

  a James Bond party .

b) A new topic begins on line

  _____.

c) The new topic is

  _____.

d) There should be a new paragraph here because

  _____.

2 Read the e-mail below. Break it up into two paragraphs.
Mark // where the new paragraph should begin.

Mail Message

Send Save Attach file

Dear M
We can have the hall in the sports
centre from 4.00 pm onwards. That
gives us plenty of time to set out the
tables and decorate the place. I have
managed to get six life-size cardboard
James Bonds to stand around the
room. We will have lots of balloons and
streamers, and the florists Bud and
Bloom are going to give us two large
arrangements. Afterwards we will need to be out of the building by midnight
or have to pay an extra £100. The party will stop at 11.00 p.m. and then we'll
have to get cracking with the black bin bags clearing everything away.
Best wishes
Q

---

3 Read the letter below and then answer the question that follows.

7 Goldfinger Drive	line 1
Tiffany	line 2
JA1 1WS	line 3
January 24th 2007	line 4
	line 5

Dear Penny Money

Thanks for agreeing to do the disco for us at this year's Cancer Research Charity *(line 6)*
party. This is just to confirm that it will be held on July 7th 2007 in the Events *(line 7)*
Room at the Nightingale Sports Centre on Darkling Road, Hampstead. The theme *(line 8)*
is James Bond, so would it be possible to play some of the famous songs from the *(line 9)*
films? My daughter's 21st birthday is on October 3rd. Are you free that evening? *(line 10)*
She is going to have a big party with a disco. Please let me know. *(line 11)*

Thank you, *(line 12)*

Cat Galore *(line 13)*

Which of these statements is correct?

A There should be a new paragraph on line 8, because it mentions the theme of the disco. ☐

B There should be a new paragraph on line 10, because it mentions a different party. ☐

C There is no need to add any new paragraphs to this letter. ☐

D There should be a new paragraph on line 10, because you shouldn't have more than four lines in one paragraph. ☐

5

Test your skills

Use the test below to find out how well you have mastered the skills in Section E.

These questions are all about the text opposite.

⊙ See the Hot Topics CD-ROM for more tips and practice on using capital letters, knowing where to put a full stop to make two sentences and using question marks correctly.

1 Why does the word *Fifteen* begin with a capital letter in line 1?

A ☐ It is the beginning of a new sentence.

B ☐ It is the start of a question.

C ☐ It is part of the title of an organisation.

D ☐ It is a mistake.

2 In which line is there a word that should **not** begin with a capital letter?

A ☐ line 5

B ☐ line 10

C ☐ line 13

D ☐ line 16

3 Which lines have an incomplete sentence?

A ☐ lines 4–5

B ☐ lines 7–8

C ☐ lines 10–11

D ☐ lines 16–17

4 Which line has a missing question mark?

A ☐ line 3

B ☐ line 7

C ☐ line 15

D ☐ line 20

5 Where would you divide the third paragraph into two paragraphs?

A ☐ line 13

B ☐ line 15

C ☐ line 17

D ☐ line 18

Check your answers.
How many did you get right? ☐ /5

Now fill your score in the chart on pages 94–95.

Test tip

In the test you'll be asked where to divide a long sentence into two.
Never split it after a joining word, e.g. *We need to stay near Bexham so. We can go to the Festival.* ✗
Never split it after a comma that is separating off part of the information, e.g. *The best campsite, which is near the beach. Must not be too far from the festival.* ✗

Could You Work at Jamie Oliver's Fifteen Restaurant?

Jamie Oliver set up The Fifteen Foundation so that disadvantaged young people aged 16–24 could turn their lives around while being trained to work in the restaurant industry.

line 1
line 2
line 3

The students who get picked to go on his course have some unusual qualifications. They must be unemployed and have had setbacks in life. This might be homelessness, drug or alcohol problems, being in trouble with the police or having done time. Many of the students finished school with no qualifications or dropped out before the end. They must also have a real passion for food and the drive and determination to get through the tough course. Need to live near enough to one of the restaurants to be able to get to work!

line 4
line 5
line 6
line 7
line 8
line 9
line 10
line 11

Says Jamie: 'Having not been the brightest banana in the bunch myself, I realised that my biggest weapon in life was the determination, enthusiasm, hands-on and 'actions speak louder than words' approach my father taught me, and I wanted to get this across to others, especially those interested in food.' On the course students work in some of the Top restaurants, study at catering college and go on trips to see how the best food is grown and produced. The highlight of the course is three days in Tuscany with Jamie Oliver learning about Italian cooking.

line 12
line 13
line 14
line 15
line 16
line 17
line 18
line 19

Would you like to know more. Then go to the Fifteen website.

line 20

F Using good grammar

By the end of this section you should understand the importance of using correct grammar. You will be able to spot when a sentence does not make sense because:

▸▸ it refers to the wrong time, e.g.

Yesterday I will go shopping. ✗

Yesterday I went shopping. ✓

▸▸ it hasn't been written correctly for the number of people doing the action, e.g.

We was furious. ✗

We were furious. ✓

1 Using the right tense

🔖 First read this ...

The verbs (action words) in a sentence must refer to the correct time when things happened – the *past*, *present* or *future*.

Read each sentence and ask yourself: '*Is this happening in the past, present or future?*' E.g.
He <u>loves</u> the funfair. (This refers to the **present**.)
He <u>loved</u> the funfair. (This refers to the **past**.)
He <u>will love</u> the funfair. (This refers to the **future**.)

▸▸ Now try it!

1 Decide whether these sentences are referring to the *present*, *past* or *future*. (Circle) the correct time in each case.

a) We finally arrived at Baxton Heights at 11.00 p.m. *present / past / future*

b) There are lots of rides I want to go on. *present / past / future*

c) They will be putting in a really scary roller coaster ride later on this year. *present / past / future*

d) We could not wait to try the 'Night Fright'. *present / past / future*

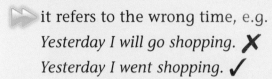

Test tip

Think: is it happening now, has it already happened or will it happen in the future?

Once you decide which it is, you will know which tense is correct.

2 Think about the time that each sentence is referring to. Write a correct version of each sentence by changing the **action word**. The first one has been done for you.

a) Yesterday he visits his sister.

   Yesterday he visited his sister.

b) At the moment I was too busy.

   _____

c) Nasim did it next week.

   _____

d) For the last three years, we will visit Drayford Theme Park.

   _____

Read this magazine letter and answer the questions about the missing words below.

> **I was nearly struck by lightning on holiday**
>
> I was on holiday with my family in France and we _____ in a house with a pool.
>
> One hot day my brother and I decided to take a dip in the swimming pool. After a couple of minutes he got out because the water _____ so cold, but I stayed in, lying in our rubber dinghy.
>
> Out of nowhere I heard a clap of thunder. Then a bolt of lightning suddenly hit a tree 10 metres away, and it went up in flames. I was petrified. I couldn't get to the edge of the pool and _____ screaming. Mum grabbed a stick and pulled the boat to the edge. I was so scared. If the lightning had been any closer, I could have died.

3 The missing word or words in the first paragraph should be:

   A will stay ☐   B were staying ☐

   C are staying ☐   D stay ☐

4 The missing word or words in the second paragraph should be:

   A is ☐   B are ☐

   C was ☐   D will be ☐

5 The missing word or words in the third paragraph should be:

   A started ☐   B starting ☐

   C start ☐   D was starting ☐

First read this ...

Check that the way the sentence is written is right for the number of people doing the action.

- Find the verb (action word).
  E.g. *eating, have to sing*

- Decide how many people or things are doing the action.

- Check whether the verb is written in the right way for that number of people.
  E.g. *He was eating* ice cream. ✓
  He were eating ice cream. ✗

Test tip

- Be careful with words like 'government' and 'committee'. These are singular but they can sound like plural words because they involve lots of people: *'The government has decided ...'*, not *'The government have decided...'*.

- Make sure you match up the correct number of people or things with the verb. Do not be confused by other singular or plural words in the sentence: *The room, which contains two beds, has a green carpet.* Remember that if two singular things are doing one action the verb needs to be plural: *The sports club and the music society are meeting tomorrow.*

Now try it!

1 Tick the correct version of each sentence.

   a) They were eating ice cream.

   They was eating ice cream.

   b) Listen to what I says to you.

   Listen to what I am saying to you.

   c) We were picked up by Dad at 9.30.

   We was picked up by Dad at 9.30.

   d) The house, which had two doors, were built of brick.

   The house, which had two doors, was built of brick.

2 The verbs in each sentence below are underlined. Note how many people are doing the action in each case. The first two have been done for you.

   A Danny Breaker, aged 30, <u>is playing</u> football for England.   _1_

   b) Adam and Eva <u>come</u> from a very talented family.   _2_

   c) Adam Stone, brother of Eva, <u>sang</u> well on *Stars in Their Eyes*.   ___

   d) Jonno Becks <u>is</u> lead singer of Famous Wannabe.   ___

   e) The host of Star Wars, on BBC1, <u>is going to be</u> Ed Less.   ___

   f) Danny, Adam and Jonno <u>are going to be</u> guests on the show.   ___

   g) The winner, who will have to be very talented, <u>will get to perform</u> live at a major concert.   ___

3   Find and (circle) the verb in each sentence below. Then
note how many people are doing the action. If the
sentence is correct, tick it. If not, put a cross. The first
one has been done for you.

there is more than one contestant so 'have' is right.

a) In round one, contestants (have) to sing
a Madonna song.   ✓

b) Unfortunately Danny Breaker sound more like the
footballer Maradona.   ☐

c) Adam and Jonno was winners.   ☐

d) In round two they have to dance and sing in a
West End musical.   ☐

When Adam Stone, in a sparkling
gold suit, walks on stage the fans
cheers. But as he sing 'Memories'
they start laughing. He cannot
reach the high notes. Jonno Becks
is better but when he dance he
slips over and knocks down part of
the scenery. At the end of round
two they has drawn.

In the final round Adam and
Jonno have to sing their own
version of the national anthem live
at an Elton John Concert. What
they don't know is that members
of the royal family are in the
audience. They is not amused, but
everyone else are. Jonno Becks
wins the prize and performs 'Star
Maker' with Famous Wannabe.

4   Read the text above. Draw a (circle) round the verbs that
are incorrect in the first paragraph.

5   In the second paragraph, which sentence is incorrect?

A first   ☐   B second   ☐

C third   ☐   D fourth   ☐

3 Test your skills

Use the test below to find out how well you have mastered the skills in Section F.

⊙ See the Hot Topics CD-ROM for more tips and practice on using tenses, on subject–verb agreement and on the verbs *to be* and *to have*.

1   In the memo below there is a grammatical error on:

A ☐ line 1

B ☐ line 2

C ☐ line 3

D ☐ line 4

▰▰▰ Memo ▰▰▰

To: Youth Work Leaders
From: Cyril Weston
Subject: *Choco* prize
Date: Jan 12th

Choco, the chocolate factory based in Northtown, has offered a free 'tour   line 1
and taste' trip to 30 young people aged between 14–18. Bexley County   line 2
Council and Bexley Youth Services Department is offering to sponsor the   line 3
cost of return coach travel. Places on the trip will be awarded to winners of line 4
the 'Bexley Pick Up Litter Competition'.   line 5

---

2   In the draft advertisement below there is a grammatical error on:

A ☐ line 1

B ☐ line 3

C ☐ line 5

D ☐ line 7

Love chocolate? *Hate litter?*

Well, you could win a fabulous 'tour   line 1
and taste' trip to *Choco* if you can   line 2
draw a winning poster to help stop   line 3
people dropping litter and spoiling   line 4
our lovely county. Draw, colour or   line 5
paint your picture on a sheet of A4   line 6
paper and sends it to: line 7

Bexley Pick Up Litter Competition,   line 8
101 Peace Drive, Bexley BX1 3RU   line 9

Closing date: March 31st   line 10

3   In the memo below there is a grammatical error on:

A ☐   line 1

B ☐   line 2

C ☐   line 3

D ☐   line 4

▰▰▰ **Memo** ▰▰▰

To: Youth Work Leaders

From: Cyril Weston

Subject: Not enough drawings for Pick Up Litter Competition

Date: May 20th

Please advertise the competition and get lots of young people to enter. Tell	line 1
them they have a good chance of winning a prize. So far we has only had three	line 2
entries. It would be very embarrassing if we could not fill the coach to take	line 3
Choco up on the offer. Maxwell Coaches will drive us there and back for free.	line 4

---

4   In the text below, which of these words should be used to fill in the gap in line 2?

A ☐   are going

B ☐   will go

C ☐   go

D ☐   went

Competition is rubbish claims coach company

30 winners of the Bexley Pick Up Litter Competition	line 1
_____ on a free 'tour and taste' trip to the	line 2
Choco factory in Northtown yesterday. But after the	line 3
trip the coach driver, Ben Maxley, said: 'I have never	line 4
had so much rubbish left on my coach before. We	line 5
were knee deep in chocolate bar wrappers, empty	line 6
cans and litter, and the kids were so hyper from	line 7
having all that sugar they kept running up and down	line 8
the coach and shrieking.'	line 9
	line 10

Check your answers.
How many did you get right?   ☐ /4

Now fill your score in the chart on pages 94–95.

Test tip

In the test you are often asked to spot mistakes involving the verbs 'to have' (*have, has, had*) and 'to be' (*am, is, are, was, were*). It is easy to get these wrong so look out for them in the test and in your own writing too.

G Preparing for the test

This section will help you to make good use of your skills when you are sitting the test.

You will find out more about:

▷▷ what a typical test question looks like

▷▷ how to answer a multiple-choice question

▷▷ how to tackle different types of questions.

1 How to answer multiple-choice questions

⏸ First read this ...

Before you sit the test you should:
- know roughly what the questions and text will look like and what you have to do
- understand how a multiple-choice question works.

▶ Now try it!

A Find out what a typical multiple-choice question looks like. Read the text and question below and the labels. Then find and tick the correct answer.

> *This tells you about the text you are going to read. It is important to know what type of text it is to be able to answer these questions.*

> *The questions may ask you to look at specific lines so each line of the text is numbered to help you find your way around.*

Questions 1–3 are about this description of the first day Billie met her dog Sam.

When I saw Sam I was amazed at how white his sharp	line 1
teeth were – they looked just like bleached cotton. For	line 2
some reason I had expected them to be yellow. But then,	line 3
I don't know much about dogs.	line 4
After he had jumped up and tried to knock me over Sam	line 5
settled down for a few moments, but then he started to	line 6
try and round us all up. I suppose his years as a sheep	line 7
dog made him uncomfortable with us walking so slowly	line 8
and aimlessly down the High Street.	line 9

1 What did the writer find most surprising about Sam's teeth?

A ☐ They are sharp.

B ☐ They are as soft as cotton.

C ☐ They are yellow.

D ☐ They are white.

> *Each question has four possible answers. Only one of them is right but the other three may appear to be right if you do not read them carefully enough. Make sure you check all four answers before deciding which is right, and don't just guess – work it out!*

B Notice that multiple-choice questions can start in two ways:

■ as a question, like Question 1:
What did the writer find most surprising about Sam's teeth?

Or
■ as the beginning of a sentence with each answer offering a different way of ending it, as in Question 2 below.

Test tip

Always follow these steps to answer a question:

1 Look at the headings and subheadings in the text.

2 Look at the question and possible answers.

3 Read the text.

4 Reread the text, paragraph by paragraph, thinking as you read. Then return to the question and make sure you follow any line numbers given in it.

5 Find the right answer. Ask yourself: *'Does the answer make sense? Is it the best match?'*

C Now read the description on page 76 again and answer Question 2.

> **2** Sam rounded up Billie and her friends because:
>
> A ☐ he had finished trying to knock them over
> B ☐ they were not moving fast enough
> C ☐ they were going along the high street
> D ☐ he was a dog.

D Read the description on page 76 again, then read the question below. Underline the line in the description that has the right answer. Then tick the correct answer below.

> **3** Which statement best describes the way Billie was moving down the High Street?
>
> A ☐ Very quickly and purposefully.
> B ☐ Slowly and without a real sense of direction.
> C ☐ Quickly but with no real sense of direction
> D ☐ Very slowly but carefully.

E Use what you have learnt to help you answer these multiple-choice questions. Questions 4–7 are about the memo below.

For each question try to decide exactly what the question is asking you to do. Is it asking you to identify the main point of the article? Is it asking you to find numbers or punctuation? Is it telling you to look at a particular sentence or specific lines?

Memo

To: All staff

From: Head of Environmental Health

Subject: Music used to rid areas of hooligan gangs

Date: July 18th

Today there has been a story in a national newspaper	line 1
describing an unusual way of ridding an area of hooligans. In	line 2
Sydney, Australia, loud speakers have been set up in streets	line 3
where youths have been gathering in large numbers and	line 4
creating a nuisance. Then, on Fridays, Saturdays and Sundays,	line 5
between 9 p.m. and 12 a.m., Barry Manilow's greatest hits have	line 6
been played loudly and non-stop. The playlist has included	line 7
Copacabana, Mandy, I Write the Songs, Can't Smile Without You	line 8
and *Looks Like We Made It.*	line 9
This method has been very effective. In one case it caused	line 10
youths to stop gathering at a railway station. It also worked in	line 11
a residential area where youths had been meeting to race cars	line 12
and bikes with their stereos blaring. However, residents have	line 13
complained at being unable to get to sleep and at having to	line 14
put up with the non-stop music.	line 15
In Tuesday's meeting I should like us to discuss:	line 16
• Is this something we should consider trying out?	line 17
• Where should we try it first?	line 18
• Should we use the same music?	line 19

4 Why did the Sydney authorities play Barry Manilow's songs?

A ☐ To help the young people gathering in the area enjoy themselves.

B ☐ To drown out the sound of the stereos coming from the cars and bikes as they raced.

C ☐ To annoy the gathered youth and make them choose to leave the area.

D ☐ To help local residents get to sleep.

5 Words and phrases in line 8 have been put in italics:

A ☐ because they are song titles

B ☐ because they are items in a list

C ☐ to persuade the members of staff to choose these songs

D ☐ because Barry Manilow would like them to be written like this.

6 How well has the scheme worked in Australia?

A ☐ Residents have loved it but it has not always got rid of the hooligans.

B ☐ It has got rid of the hooligans but some residents have been unhappy.

C ☐ It has worked well for everybody.

D ☐ The scheme has not got rid of the hooligans and it has annoyed residents.

7 The Head of Environmental Health wants his staff to:

A ☐ read the national newspaper reports about how the scheme has worked in Australia

B ☐ listen to Barry Manilow music

C ☐ play Barry Manilow music to residents

D ☐ discuss whether they should play Barry Manilow music in areas troubled by hooligans.

Test tip

■ Don't be put off if you aren't sure of an answer to one question in the test. The answer to the next question never relies on you having got the first question right!

■ If you have searched really carefully for the right answer but still can't find it then do not leave the answer space blank. Decide which of the possible answers are definitely wrong. Then choose the answer you think is closest to being right. In the onscreen test you can mark a question for review so that you can return to it at the end – but make sure you leave yourself time to do this.

What the question is asking for

First read this ...

When you read a question you need to be sure that you understand what you are being asked to do and which reading skills will help you to answer the question.

Making sense of a question

- ■ Read it through several times.

- ■ Identify the important words that show exactly what you have to do.

- ■ Keep asking yourself: 'What have I got to find out?' E.g. <u>What</u> is <u>the main point</u> of the <u>leaflet</u>?

> *I need to sum up the big idea that the leaflet is telling readers.*

Now try it!

A Study each of the questions below. <u>Underline</u> their key words. Then match each one with the correct answer by drawing a line across.

a) How many people bought the game?

> I need to choose a heading.

b) What is the main point in the second paragraph?

> I need to sum up the second paragraph.

c) Which of the following list of possible headings would be best for this report?

> I need to work out what the writer wants to express to readers.

d) Why did the writer leave his job?

> I need to find a number.

e) What is the purpose of this leaflet?

> I need to search for a reason.

B Read each question in the list below. Work out what it is asking you to do. Decide which group of questions it belongs to. Write its letter in the correct box.

List of questions

a) What is the <u>main point of the leaflet</u>?

b) In which year did Jack start his business?

c) What is the main idea in the fifth paragraph?

d) Which ingredients are used to make potato crisps?

e) What is the main work of a firefighter?

f) The best title for the leaflet would be ...

1 These questions want you to think about the whole text.

a)

2 These questions want you to think about a paragraph or small chunk of the text.

Groups of questions

3 These questions ask you to find one word or a few details in a text.

g) How many people attended the match on July 23rd 2006?

h) Who was the first person to win one million pounds?

i) Which of these subheadings would be best for the first paragraph?

j) Why are the points under the subheading listed in this order?

k) Without changing the meaning in line 6, 'dark' could best be replaced by ...

l) What is the purpose of this leaflet?

C We're now going to focus on how different reading skills will help you answer the questions. Questions 1–4 are about the leaflet opposite.

- ■ Read the Test tip.
- ■ Then read the title of the text.
- ■ Next read the questions.
- ■ Then read the text and work out the right answer to each question and tick the correct box.

1 What is the purpose of the leaflet?

- A ☐ To warn readers how dangerous sunbathing is.
- B ☐ To help readers work out what clothes to wear in the sun.
- C ☐ To advise readers how to keep healthy in hot summer weather.
- D ☐ To persuade readers to drink lots of water.

To work out the purpose I need to work out what the whole text is about. So I need to:
- • skim the text
- • keep stopping to ask 'What is this about?'
- • at the end ask 'What message is the writer trying to give readers?'

2 Which of these will help keep you cool?

- A ☐ Applying lots of sun cream.
- B ☐ Wearing a hat and sunglasses.
- C ☐ Wearing cotton or silk clothes.
- D ☐ Avoiding fizzy drinks.

To find things that will help keep someone cool, I need to:
- • scan to see where each of the answers is given in the text
- • read that part carefully to see if it is about keeping cool or not.

3 What is <u>the main idea</u> in the first bullet point?

- A ☐ To sell sun cream to readers.
- B ☐ To explain how sun cream works.
- C ☐ To advise readers to use sun cream properly.
- D ☐ To warn readers of the danger of sunburn.

4 Read lines 18–19. Why should you add a pinch of salt and sugar to drinks?

- A ☐ Doctors add it to their drinks.
- B ☐ It makes the drink last longer.
- C ☐ Your body loses salts in hot weather.
- D ☐ It makes the drinks taste better.

Summer Sun Safety

Follow these tips to help you stay happy and safe even when temperatures soar.   line 1

✴ Put on lots of high factor sun cream all over every part of your body that will   line 2
be exposed to the sun. Make sure you apply it at least 20 minutes before you   line 3
go out. Apply more sun cream after you have swum. Make sure you don't   line 4
stay out in the sun too long for your skin type – you can still burn even with   line 5
sun cream on.   line 6

✴ Wear a hat and sunglasses whenever you go out in the sun. Loose, light   line 7
coloured clothing made in natural fabrics like cotton and silk will help keep   line 8
you cool.   line 9

✴ Stay out of the sun between 11.00 a.m. and 3.00 p.m. – the hottest part of   line 10
the day.   line 11

✴ Sitting in the shade does not mean those sun rays won't get to you. Always   line 12
apply lots of sun cream even if you are sitting out in the shade under a tree,   line 13
or parasol.   line 14

✴ Make sure you drink plenty of water. It's much better for you than fizzy drinks   line 15
or straight fruit juice but if you don't like it plain then try adding water to   line 16
squash or fruit juice, eat jelly or even make and munch some ice lollies!   line 17

✴ It's easy to lose vital body salts in hot weather so some doctors recommend   line 18
adding a pinch of salt and a pinch of sugar to drinks.   line 19

D Questions 5–9 are all about the information text opposite.

- Read the Test tip which explains the focus of these questions – questions that are worded negatively.
- Then read the title of the text.
- Next read the questions.
- Then read the text and work out the right answer to each question and tick the correct box.

5 Cheshire cheese is <u>not</u> made in:

A ☐ pale yellow

B ☐ blue

C ☐ red

D ☐ green.

6 Cheshire cheese does <u>not</u>:

A ☐ take four weeks to mature

B ☐ crumble easily

C ☐ have a soft and creamy texture

D ☐ taste salty.

7 Which of these would <u>not</u> be a good subheading for the third paragraph?

A ☐ Different types of Cheshire Cheese

B ☐ Only buy Cheshire Cheese

C ☐ Some facts about how Cheshire Cheese is made

D ☐ The different qualities of Cheshire cheese

8 This information text includes each of these facts except:

A ☐ Cheshire Cheese is mentioned in the Domesday book.

B ☐ Cheshire Cheese is made from milk that comes from cows feeding on pasture land that gets its water from salty springs.

C ☐ Cheshire Cheese is the UK's favourite cheese.

D ☐ Cheshire Cheese is less salty than Feta cheese.

Test tip

Some questions ask you to spot which answer is **not** present in the text or **not** true about the text.

E.g. *Which colour is Cheshire cheese <u>not</u> made in?*
A pale yellow
B blue
C red
D green.

You have to be very careful not to be caught out by these questions. To tackle this sort of question you need to:

- scan the text to find out whether each possible answer can be found in the text or pictures or is true about the text, e.g. *Is there any pale yellow Cheshire Cheese? – Yes, it is in the picture.*
Red and blue Cheshire Cheese are mentioned in the text.

- choose the answer that is not found in the text or pictures or is not true about the text.

Delicious Cheshire delight

Cheshire is thought to be Britain's oldest named cheese. It was first mentioned in the Domesday Book at the end of the 11th century, but is believed to date back to Roman Britain.

line 1
line 2
line 3
line 4

Today about 6,500 tonnes of Cheshire cheese are sold every year, making it the UK's most popular crumbly cheese. Traditional manufacturing methods are still used, with open vats and manual curd handling.

line 5
line 6
line 7
line 8

From start to finish it takes about four weeks to mature the cheese, which has a fresh milky taste and an open crumbly texture. More aged varieties have more complex flavours and are firmer. Along with the traditional pale Cheshire cheese, there is a red variety coloured with annatto which is also used in Red Leicester, and a blue, which is punctured during the curing process. Its distinctive flavour is due to the salt springs which run under much of the pasture land and which give a salty tang to the milk the cheese is made from. But Cheshire usually has half the salt content of Feta cheese.

line 9
line 10
line 11
line 12
line 13
line 14
line 15
line 16
line 17
line 18
line 19
line 20

The British Cheese Board has a number of recipes using Cheshire cheese at its website: www.cheshirecheese.org.

line 21
line 22

3 Answering questions on vocabulary, grammar, punctuation and spelling

This unit shows you how to recognise and answer questions that check you can:

▷ understand the meaning of a word

▷ use correct punctuation and grammar in your writing

▷ spot spelling mistakes.

Vocabulary

First read this ...

It is important to have a wide vocabulary and the test will be asking you questions to see how wide your vocabulary is. The test does this in different ways, as you will see in what you are about to do.

> **Test tip**
>
> When a question asks about the meaning of a word, you need to:
>
> ■ scan the text to find where the word or phrase belongs in the text
>
> ■ carefully read the sentence and paragraph it is part of, so you know what it means
>
> ■ check for words that you know can be spelt more than one way, e.g. *to/too/two*
>
> ■ keep asking yourself: *'What should that word mean? Is it spelt the right way?'*

Now try it!

A Questions 1–4 are about the draft advertisement below.
Follow the advice above as you answer them.

Do you like to get out and about rather than being stuck indoors?	line 1
Do you know your local area 'like the back of your hand'?	line 2
Would you like to earn good money?	line 3
Have you past your driving test?	line 4
A local company needs hard-working, polite couriers to pick up and deliver	line 5
light packages to customers all over your area quickly and efficiently.	line 6
Full-time and _____ hours available. Know experience needed as full	line 7
training will be given. Interested? Phone Baz on 01854 785899.	line 8

1 Which of these phrases in lines 1–4 contains a word that is used incorrectly?

A ☐ out and about

B ☐ like the back of your hand

C ☐ would you like to earn good money

D ☐ past your driving test.

2 Which of these words from lines 6–8 is used incorrectly?

A ☐ light

B ☐ quickly

C ☐ efficiently

D ☐ know.

3 Without changing the meaning, 'couriers' in line 5 could best be replaced by:

A ☐ adults

B ☐ security guards

C ☐ delivery personnel

D ☐ map readers.

4 The word which would best fill the space on line 7 is:

A ☐ part-time

B ☐ long

C ☐ short-time

D ☐ daylight.

Grammar

When a test question asks you to search a draft text for a grammar mistake, you need to look for a sentence where:

■ the wrong part of a verb has been used, e.g.
The two bakers <u>has</u> to be able to make all kinds of bread. ✗
The two bakers <u>have</u> to be able to make all kinds of bread. ✔

■ the wrong tense of the verb has been used, e.g.
The wages will be £6.20 per hour and shifts <u>were</u>
4.00 a.m.–11.00 a.m. Mon–Sat. ✗
The wages will be £6.20 per hour and shifts <u>will be</u>
4.00 a.m.–11.00 a.m. Mon–Sat. ✔

■ a word is not plural or singular when it needs to be, e.g.
We make <u>lot</u> of different kinds of bread. ✗
We make <u>lots</u> of different kinds of bread. ✔

Now try it!

A Use what you have learnt to help you answer these multiple-choice questions. Questions 5 and 6 are based on the draft memo below.

Memo ....

To:	All catering staff	line 1
From:	Head of Personnel	line 2
Subject:	Hand washing and cleaning of all surfaces	line 3

Over the last month there has been a dramatic rises in the | line 4
number of staff taking days off because they say they have | line 5
food poisoning. Therefore we wish to remind all catering | line 6
staff that it is vital that they: | line 7

● Wash their hands thoroughly before handling any food | line 8

● Wash their hands after handling raw meat or fish | line 9

● Wash their hands before touching vegetables or fruit | line 10

● Clean all work surfaces before and after preparing food | line 11

● Had long hair tied back, and wear the catering uniform | line 12
and hat. | line 13

5 There is a grammatical error on:

A ☐ line 4
B ☐ line 5
C ☐ line 6
D ☐ line 7

6 In which other line did the writer also make a grammatical error?

A ☐ line 8
B ☐ line 9
C ☐ line 11
D ☐ line 12

Punctuation

First read this ...

Test questions checking your understanding of punctuation will ask you to read a draft text and notice where punctuation has been:

■ left out

■ added where it is not needed.

Test tip

These are the kinds of punctuation mistakes you need to be able to spot:

■ a capital letter has not been used to begin a proper noun (*jason*) or has been incorrectly used to start a common noun (*ready salted Crisps*)

■ a question mark is missing from the end of a question, e.g. *Will you help*

■ a sentence is incomplete, e.g. *At 9.00 p.m. on Friday we*

■ two sentences have been run together and they need to be split, e.g. *My Dad said I can have a small party. H/He is going out for the evening.*

■ A new paragraph is needed because it starts a new topic, e.g. *The next point on our list is where to hold the concert.*

A Use what you have learnt to help you answer these multiple choice questions. Questions 7–12 are about the e-mail below.

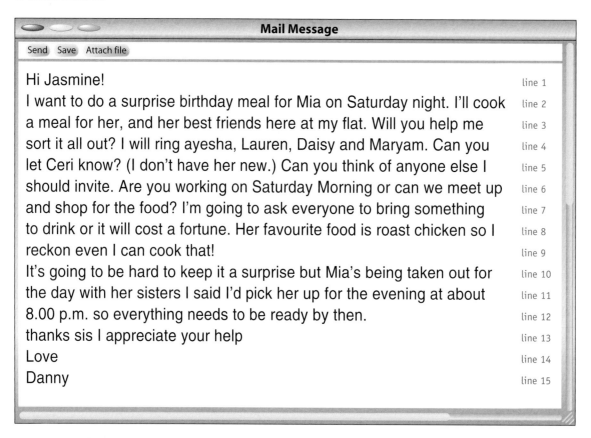

Mail Message

Send Save Attach file

Hi Jasmine! — line 1
I want to do a surprise birthday meal for Mia on Saturday night. I'll cook — line 2
a meal for her, and her best friends here at my flat. Will you help me — line 3
sort it all out? I will ring ayesha, Lauren, Daisy and Maryam. Can you — line 4
let Ceri know? (I don't have her new.) Can you think of anyone else I — line 5
should invite. Are you working on Saturday Morning or can we meet up — line 6
and shop for the food? I'm going to ask everyone to bring something — line 7
to drink or it will cost a fortune. Her favourite food is roast chicken so I — line 8
reckon even I can cook that! — line 9
It's going to be hard to keep it a surprise but Mia's being taken out for — line 10
the day with her sisters I said I'd pick her up for the evening at about — line 11
8.00 p.m. so everything needs to be ready by then. — line 12
thanks sis I appreciate your help — line 13
Love — line 14
Danny — line 15

7 Which word in lines 2–4 should have a capital letter?

A ☐ birthday
B ☐ meal
C ☐ best
D ☐ ayesha

8 In which line is there a word that should not have a capital letter?

A ☐ line 1
B ☐ line 5
C ☐ line 6
D ☐ line 11

9 On which line is there an incomplete sentence?

A ☐ line 4
B ☐ line 5
C ☐ line 6
D ☐ line 7

10 The writer should have begun a new paragraph on:

A ☐ line 3
B ☐ line 5
C ☐ line 6
D ☐ line 9

11 A question mark has been missed out on:

A ☐ line 4
B ☐ line 5
C ☐ line 6
D ☐ line 11

12 Which of the following needs to be added to the sentence on line 11?

A ☐ A full stop.
B ☐ An exclamation mark.
C ☐ A capital letter, a comma and a full stop.
D ☐ A capital letter and a comma.

Spelling

In the test you may be asked to:

- spot spelling mistakes
- choose the correct spelling of a word.

Test tip

Spotting spelling mistakes is *tricky for everyone* even good spellers, so take your time.

- Read each line you have to check slowly and carefully.
- Sound out each part of every word you have to look at.
- Think about whether the spelling and the meaning of the word is right, e.g. *to/too/two*.

Now try it!

A Use what you have learnt to help you answer these multiple-choice questions. Questions 13–18 are about the memo below.

To: Fun Time Catering Team	line 1
From: E Ting	line 2
Subject: Wedsday's Gala Dinner	line 3

As you are all aware over 100 famous sports celebrities will be attending this   line 4
event therefore it is very important that we impress them with our food and   line 5
serviss. Even though these clients have used us in the passed there is no   line 6
guarantee they will do so again. The competition is _____ so we have to make   line 7
sure they now we are still the best.   line 8

All the food is on a sporting theme. As guests arrive they will be offered drinks and   line 9
small eats that are set out on round trays in the patern of a dartboard. Guests will   line 10
be encouraged to pick up their food with a 'dart'.   line 11

When guests sit down to dinner the starter will be 'skittle chicken'. Each plate will   line 12
be made to look like a ten pin bowling alley. The chicken bites will be the pins,   line 13
with cherry tomato bowls and vegetable strip alleys.   line 14

The main course will be a series of dishes made to look like racing cars. These   line 15
will be laid out across a starting line witch stretches across each table. Servers   line 16
will wave a chequered flag when all the dishes have been laid on a table.   line 17

The puddings will include pairs of mango sorbet ice skates, chocolate discus, and   line 18
gold _____ iced cakes.   line 19

13 On which of these lines is there a spelling mistake?

A ☐ line 3

B ☐ line 5

C ☐ line 7

D ☐ line 8

14 Which word is incorrectly spelt on lines 5–6?

A ☐ therefore

B ☐ important

C ☐ impress

D ☐ serviss

15 The missing word on line 8 should be spelt:

A ☐ toff

B ☐ tuff

C ☐ tough

D ☐ touff

16 There is a spelling mistake on:

A ☐ line 10

B ☐ line 12

C ☐ line 13

D ☐ line 14

17 Which word is incorrectly spelt on line 6?

A ☐ round

B ☐ patern

C ☐ dartboard

D ☐ guests

18 How should the missing word on line 19 be spelt?

A ☐ meddle

B ☐ medol

C ☐ medal

D ☐ medel

Track your progress

Write the date when you completed each unit, and tick to show whether you'd like more practice or whether you're happy with your skills in each unit. Don't forget to add your score from the end of section tests, and add up your total score at the end!

Section A: Ways of reading

Unit	Skills covered	Date	I'd like more practice with this	I'm OK with this	End of section test score
1	Scanning				
2	Skimming				
3	Reading carefully				
4	Working out what a word means				
5	Identifying the main point of a paragraph				
6	Identifying details in texts				
7	All Section A skills				/5

Section B: Understanding how texts are organised

Unit	Skills covered	Date	I'd like more practice with this	I'm OK with this	End of section test score
1	Identifying e-mails, letters, memos, instructions, charts and adverts				
2	Identifying headings, subheadings, paragraphs and numbered/bulleted points				
3	Finding information in lists				
4	Reading charts and tables				
5	Reading texts that include images and symbols				
6	All Section B skills				/4

Section C: Understanding what writers want their readers to do

Unit	Skills covered	Date	I'd like more practice with this	I'm OK with this	End of section test score
1	Identifying information, instruction, description and persuasive texts				
2	Understanding how instruction texts are organised				
3	Understanding the features and language of description texts				
4	Understanding the features and language of explanation texts				
5	Understanding the features and language of persuasive texts				
6	Understanding the differences between formal and informal				
7	Identifying formal and informal writing and using each appropriately				
8	All Section C skills				/4